DOCUMENTS OF MODERN HISTORY

General Editors:

A. G. Dickens
Director, Institute of Historical Research,
University of London

Alun Davies
Professor of Modern History,
University College of Swansea

Post-War Integration in Europe

Richard Vaughan

Professor of History, University of Hull

EDWARD ARNOLD

First published 1976 by
Edward Arnold (Publishers) Ltd
25 Hill Street, London W1X 8LL

ISBN cloth: 0 7131 5881 6
       paper: 0 7131 5882 4

cc .

Printed in Great Britain by
The Camelot Press Ltd, Southampton

Contents

VII   The Common Market since 1960   169

One day, taking its pattern from the United States of America, there will be founded the United States of Europe.

George Washington

I represent a party which does not yet exist—civilization. This party will make the twentieth century. There will issue from it first the United States of Europe and later the United States of the World.

Victor Hugo

Acknowledgements

I gladly express my thanks to the publishers, libraries and other institutions that have given permission for material to be reproduced here or helped me to obtain it. In this last respect I would like to thank especially Professor Geoffrey Warner and the members of staff of the Brynmor Jones Library of the University of Hull, in particular Miss Wendy Mann. I wish also to thank Professor Warner and Dr Richard Mayne for kindly reading the typescript through for me and giving me the benefit of their expertise; Mr Tony Wells for his help in obtaining copies of some documents; and Mr John Davey of Edward Arnold for his invaluable assistance on the publishing side. As usual, my wife Margaret and my children have helped, in one way or another; I thank them all. I owe thanks too to the students who have followed my course on post-war European integration in the last two years. Last, but not least, I thank Miss Susan Appleton and Mrs Alwyn Thurlow for their typing.

Abbreviations

Benelux	Belgium, the Netherlands and Luxembourg
CMEA *or* Comecon	Council for Mutual Economic Assistance
ECA	Economic Cooperation Administration
EDC	European Defence Community
EEC	European Economic Community *or* Common Market
EFTA	European Free Trade Association
EMU	Economic and Monetary Union
Euratom	European Atomic Energy Community
GATT	General Agreement on Tariffs and Trade
NATO	North Atlantic Treaty Organization
OEEC	Organization for European Economic Cooperation
UNO	United Nations Organization
WEU	Western European Union

Introduction

The real starting point for the history of European integration was the close of the Second World War. The war had, in so many different ways, wiped the slate clean: the European economy lay in ruins, disrupted, devastated; and continental Europe's political system of nation states had been almost dismantled as a result of the activities of the Third Reich. In that now distant summer of 1945 there was a feeling abroad, a restless, uneasy, notion of turning over a new leaf, of starting afresh; a stirring of the spirit which in England toppled the wartime but conservative hero Churchill and set up in his place a socialist government with a politically effective majority. Prominent in this vague striving for a new, a different, Europe, was the concept of federalism, of some kind of political union. But, though 1945 makes a realistic starting point for the historian of European integration, already before then certain vital events had occurred and certain significant doctrines had been expounded which were to have a lasting influence on post-war European integration.

The so-called European idea, in earlier times the concept of a united Christian Europe, later of a European federal union of some kind, has had numerous devotees and exponents down the centuries, including Pierre Dubois with his assembly of European princes at Toulouse around 1300, and Maximilien de Béthune, duc de Sully, more than three hundred years later, with his fifteen-state federation ruled by a Council-General. At first these ideas were universalist—Europe was conceived of as united under the universal authority of the emperor, or of the pope; or in the case of Pierre Dubois, of the Crown of France. Later, when the nation states had begun to evolve, these ideas became federalist and, by the nineteenth century, when they were widely held and publicized, they were specifically aimed at replacing the national state system and rectifying its increasingly glaring faults. The Quaker William Penn wanted a 'European Diet or Parliament' as early as 1693; in 1712 the Abbé de Saint-Pierre proposed a European Senate at Utrecht with a European army; Jeremy Bentham argued in 1787 for a Diet, a common European army and the abolition of colonies;

Rousseau had a plan for a European federation. At St Helena, Napoleon dreamed of a European federation: 'I don't think any stability can exist in Europe without the cooperation and confederation of the great peoples.' In the early nineteenth century the phrase 'United States of Europe' became as well known and as often bandied about as that other new word of those days—'nationality'. Victor Hugo used it in a famous speech at the Paris Peace Congress of 1849, and the 1867 Geneva Peace Congress gave birth to a journal called *The United States of Europe*. This long tradition of a United Europe has had great and famous exponents in our century too, perhaps most notable among them Count Coudenhove-Kalergi. His father, product of the union of a Dutch and a Greek family, was an Austro-Hungarian diplomat; his mother was Japanese. Count Sforza, Herriot, Briand, Adenauer and many others joined his Pan-European Union which was based at Vienna; his book, *Pan-Europe,* published in 1923, was translated into several languages. Coudenhove-Kalergi exercised a vital influence on the course of post-war integration in Europe through his activities as a war-time exile in the United States of America, for he was largely responsible for promoting American public opinion and alerting the American authorities in favour of a new, united, federal Europe after the war.

The growing menace of exaggerated nationalism in Italy and then Germany in the 1920s and 1930s produced a many-sided federalist reaction which contained the seeds of much post-war integration. These were the years of the Briand Plan (1); the proposed Austro-German customs union and the actual Belgian-Luxembourg union (22); the Baltic and Balkan Unions; the Oslo and Ouchy Conventions of 1930 and 1932 in which Holland and Belgium tried, with other countries, to create a customs union open to all which would entail a progressive lowering of tariffs; and much more besides.

The outcome of the Second World War placed the destiny of Europe in the hands of the two super-powers, Russia and America, and it was their confrontation in the immediate post-war years which divided Europe into two distinct blocs and kept it divided thereafter. The post-war plans and aspirations which were elaborated by the Western Allies, and, more importantly, by the Resistance Movement, incorporated a major element of federalism. Among the allied leaders, Winston Churchill repeatedly pleaded, although in the vaguest of terms, for a regional European federation, a Council of Europe as he called it in 1943; but at Teheran in November 1943 Stalin opposed Churchill's suggested confederations in Eastern and Central Europe, and the decision was taken to recreate Europe's system of independent national states, five or six of which would be fragments of the dismantled former Third Reich. Thereafter, the allies rejected federalism; most of Europe's nation states had governments in exile, waiting patiently for the opportunity to restore their national sovereignties. Even so, Benelux was devised and agreed to in 1944 (18): the governments-in-exile of Belgium, Holland and Luxembourg thereby laid a foundation for subsequent integration.

In divided post-war Europe what integration there was had perforce to come separately in East and West. In the East the rampant nationalism of the pre-war years was replaced by a savage Stalinism: integration took the form of Russian exploitation and dominance. This Soviet 'empire' has since then showed signs of serious internal weaknesses, and Comecon, which was at first a purely Russian device set up in 1949 by Stalin in part as a counter to OEEC, has achieved more by way of international cooperation especially in terms of the coordination of different specializations, than in the field of supranational integration. In the West, on the other hand, where the United States played a quite different role to that of Russia in Eastern Europe, Great Power influence was more benign, and the Marshall Plan brought about a good deal of integration, though less than its creators had hoped for.

Among the causes or impulses behind the integration which took place in Western Europe in the years after General Marshall inaugurated the European Recovery Programme in June 1947 was fear of communism; not just of Russian military power, but also of communist coups like that in Prague in 1948—after all, the domestic politics of both France and Italy were characterized after the war by massive communist parties creating, in the minds of many, just as dangerous a political problem as that presented by defeated, partitioned, Germany. Integration, then, was spurred on by this twofold fear, of the old enemy, Germany; of the new enemy, communism. It was brought about, too, by American pressure in favour of a united Europe, in part at least altruistic; it was facilitated by Europe's economic and political ruin; urged by a group of dedicated 'European' statesmen, especially Konrad Adenauer and Alcide de Gasperi, supported by a vociferous federalist lobby; encouraged above all by the French, determined to become again a major continental power, albeit in a new, European guise; and finally made useful or even necessary by technological advances of every kind, including television, the new international airlines, and automation, as well as by economic developments and requirements.

It goes without saying that, if one examines the forces exerted in favour of integration country by country, the smaller countries, like Belgium and Holland, tend to be the most committed. It was they who created Benelux; they who supported the initiatives which led to the setting up of the Common Market in 1957. The Scandinavian countries, small at any rate in terms of population, have made remarkable progress in spite of some setbacks, and they too began their integration before the creation of the European Community. The Nordic Council dates from 1952 (19); the Nordic Labour Market was created in 1954–6; and that extraordinarily successful example of international cooperation, the Scandinavian Airlines System, had been created as early as 1946. West Germany, in no sense a small power, has consistently promoted moves towards integration, perhaps in the early years because her political rehabilitation could most easily be effected by this means. France, as so often, is an enigma. Because of de Gaulle, who was in any case invariably portrayed both outside as well as inside France in an exaggerated, caricatured, image, it is too easily assumed that France has consistently opposed 'Europe'. But this is not true. Think back in history: Dubois, Sully, St Pierre were all of them French. Who said, in 1925, 'My greatest desire is to see one day appear the United States of Europe'?—Edouard Herriot, French statesman. It was the French government which sponsored the Briand Plan of 1930; the French who, in September 1947, offered to form a customs union with anyone who cared to join; the French government which put forward the historic Schuman Declaration of 9 May 1950 which led to the creation of the ECSC. And during the negotiations in 1949 which preceded the setting up of the Council of Europe some of the French argued for 'a close union between all the peoples of Europe' in the words of a French official document, as opposed to the British idea of a 'European council, appointed by and responsible to governments'.

What then of Britain? One could argue that she has, from time immemorial, opposed any sort of integration on the continent of Europe and that, since the war, she has been responsible for acting in a consistently negative way towards integration attempts. Either, as with the OEEC and the Council of Europe, she has contrived so to dilute the dose of proposed integration as to render it entirely innocuous or inoperative; or, as with the proposals for a European Army or a European Political Community (EDC and EPC), she has contributed to their abandonment. In the past she opposed the Ouchy Convention; later, she refused to take part in the creation of the ECSC and the EEC; more recently she joined the Six only to have serious second thoughts about her membership. Many of the reservations which were advanced in 1975 about Britain's continued membership of the European Community were identical to the time-honoured reasons or pretexts for her past lack of cooperation with the continental powers. These have traditionally been her connections with the Commonwealth, her leadership of the Sterling Area, her (real or imagined) 'special' relationship with the United States, and the maintenance of her coveted national sovereignty. As to the first of these, it certainly is the case that British membership of a European customs union in the 1950s would have ruined the Commonwealth's preferential tariff system; as to the last, it is a fact that every other European country—with the exception of Switzerland, Spain, Portugal, Sweden, Finland and Russia, none of them noted for enthusiasm for integration—had suffered the total demolition of its national sovereignty during or after the Second World War.

The same thrust of public opinion which made Resistance newspapers like *Het Parool* in the Netherlands and *Combat* in France thoroughly radical and federal in their political outlook continued in the years after the war, even though the federal aspirations of the Resistance had been all but ignored in the post-war reconstruction of the European system of nation states and their concomitant political parties. In 1945–47 private organizations dedicated to the federal ideal sprang up everywhere: the United Europe Movement, the European League for Economic Cooperation, the European Union of Federalists, Nouvelles Équippes Internationales. They joined the ranks of some that had existed earlier, for example the Federal Union, founded in London in 1938. This powerful stirring of public opinion came to a resounding climax in the European Congress at The Hague on 8–10 May 1948, organized by the International Committee of the Movements for European Unity which had been set up the previous December (8). Winston Churchill, the President of Honour, opened the proceedings in the Ridderzaal or Hall of the Knights in the Netherlands Parliament Building. Some 800 delegates from all parts of Western Europe attended the Congress, conspicuous among them a strong German delegation led by Konrad Adenauer. It was perhaps a portent for the future that there were practically no members of the British Labour Party, then in power at Westminster. As a result of The Hague Congress the European Movement, with a National Council in each country, was inaugurated, presided over by Léon Blum, Winston Churchill, Alcide de Gasperi and Paul Henri Spaak. The organization, which has continued ever since to foster and represent 'European' opinion, was largely responsible for the establishment in 1949 of the so-called Council of Europe, which was really—thanks very largely to the British—an emasculated version of the European Assembly proposed at The Hague, rendered permanently ineffective by a Council of Ministers placed, as it were, upon its back.

Ineffective as it proved to be, the Council of Europe, or, more accurately, its Consultative Assembly at Strasbourg, was at least a move in the direction of European unity. Moreover, many subsequent initiatives towards integration were either originated or encouraged by this Assembly. These initiatives resulted most importantly in the setting up in the 1950s of the European Coal and Steel Community, the Common Market itself (the EEC) and Euratom. Similar initiatives, for a European Army, for a European Political Union, for a European Transport Authority all fell through. Successes alternated with setbacks such as these, but, nonetheless, the achievements of the fifties in the field of integration and intergovernmental cooperation were notable. The OEEC effectively reduced non-tariff barriers to trade between its seventeen member states, even enjoying some success in the abolition of import quotas; its dependent organization, the European Payments Union, went some way towards providing a mechanism for the multilateral adjustment of payments. But attempts in 1949 and 1950 to increase the powers of OEEC to make it more effective were foiled by Britain, which preferred the Organization to remain, what it soon became, a mere information centre for economic affairs. Beside it, the ECSC and the EEC emerged in the late 1950s as more powerful, more effective and more supranational. While they continued to forge ahead with a customs union entailing the total abolition of internal tariffs, a Common Agricultural Policy, and the merging of their executives and assemblies into a single instititional structure with a single European Parliament which soon put the Strasbourg Assembly in the shade, the rest of Europe, led by the United Kingdom, sought refuge in a loosely organized free trade area—the EFTA. By 1960, Europe was divided between the Six and the Seven, and OEEC, ceasing to be a specifically European organization, was joined by Canada and the United States and transformed from the Organization for European Economic Cooperation into the Organization for Economic Cooperation and Development.

The sixties, then, witnessed everywhere in Europe the dismantling of tariff walls and, inside the European Community, important progress in the already mentioned merging of the executives and evolution of the Common Agricultural Policy. But, though the lowering of tariffs was achieved faster than had been predicted or allowed for, the merging of the executives and the Common Agricultural Policy suffered difficulties and delays. Moreover, other projected moves towards further integration in the sixties, both inside and outside the EEC, were either altogether abandoned or indefinitely postponed. The pace of the fifties slackened; the promise faded. Protests against supranationalism disturbed the superficially monolithic and conformist structure of Comecon; above all the foreign policies of France, disjointed by the eccentric old-time nationalism of de Gaulle, dangerously rocked the EEC boat and undermined the military effectiveness of NATO. De Gaulle and France continued patently to demonstrate their European mission, but it was in no sense supranational or integrationist, and the creation in 1963 of a Franco–German axis seemed a move away from the integrity of the Common Market (36). All through this decade a single directly-elected European Parliament was on the agenda of that institution but seemed further away from implementation than ever (37). Monetary union, an integrated transport policy—both of them, like the directly-elected European Parliament, laid down in the Treaty of Rome—even the much-heralded enlargement of the Community, all these were pipe-dreams, or so many dead ducks.

One explanation for this manifest retardation of the pace of integration in the sixties has been found in the changed international situation. Instead of the Cold War, there was now rapprochement between West and East: *Ostpolitik*. Instead of fear and uncertainty, security and peace. Instead of an all-powerful United States urging integration and showering Marshall Aid on Europe, a country much less politically and economically assertive. Instead of an all-powerful Soviet Union firmly in control of a unified and uniform communist bloc, whisperings of disruption, economic reform, nationalism, even rebellion. Meanwhile, Western Europe remained economically healthy so that further moves towards integration lost their urgency although the demolition of tariff walls was facilitated. The steeply upward growth curve—especially of the EEC countries—only flattened somewhat after 1965. The mass movement of immigrant labour which was the life-blood of this expanding European economy likewise continued in full flood till 1965. Thereafter it became increasingly apparent that the movement was in decline and that perhaps only one-eighth of these migrants would actually settle in their new country and thus be in any sense 'integrationist'.

A further explanation for the lull in integration in the 1960s is in terms of personalities. True, the tireless originator of the Schuman

Plan, the Common Market and the Action Committee for the United States of Europe, Jean Monnet, remained as active as ever. But the handful of statesmen who really were responsible for creating the so-called 'Little Europe' of the Six had disappeared from the scene. Konrad Adenauer, Chancellor of the Federal Republic of Germany, left office in 1963; Robert Schuman's remarkable career as Minister of Finance, of Justice, of Foreign Affairs, in successive French governments between 1946 and 1958, was crowned by his term of office as President of the European Parliament in 1958–60, but he died in 1963. Alcide de Gasperi died in 1954, a decade after he had become Italian Minister of Foreign Affairs in 1944. These men were Roman Catholics, anti-Nazi, German-speaking in the first place, and united in their European enthusiasm. The Belgian socialist and veteran Foreign Minister Paul Henri Spaak came near to these centrist politicians in his promotion of the 'European' cause and in his stature as a statesman, making a particularly important contribution in the council of OEEC, as President of the Consultative Assembly of the Council of Europe in 1949–51, and as Secretary-general of NATO in 1957–61. In the sixties there were no comparable figures, except perhaps for Walter Hallstein, the first President of the EEC Commission (1958–1967); but he lacked a national power base and international prestige. In spite of him, and others like him, Europe's governments tended to be detached and at best lukewarm to the European idea, and the European public was seldom enthusiastic.

What then, of the last five years? The outstanding fact is the enlargement of the EEC to include three new members: Great Britain, Denmark and Ireland; and the self-exclusion of a fourth, Norway. At the same time the distinction between being 'in' or 'out' has been considerably blurred by a network of trade agreements between the EEC and non-members (42). Another significant development has been the steady weighting of power in the EEC towards the intergovernmental Council of Ministers and the Permanent Representatives of the Member States in Brussels, and away from the supranational Commission. The dramatic turn-about in economic affairs which began early in 1970, the sudden appearance of world shortages of essential commodities, the so-called energy crisis, rampant inflation, growing unemployment—these events cannot be said to have resulted in any sort of 'European' response, nor in any further efforts towards integration.

The small size of this book has made it impossible to include documents illustrating what might be termed 'non-governmental' or 'unofficial' integration. Some may claim that tourism has little to do with integration; yet the astounding post-war growth of this industry or activity has greatly increased the interdependence of the European economies. Furthermore, this development has in part escaped the control of governments so that, in some measure, it can be said to be eroding national sovereignties. The same is true of the growth of the multinational companies, about which so much has been written in recent years. In 1970 the gross national products of several European countries—Denmark, Austria, Norway, for example—were smaller than the annual sales of General Motors or Standard Oil. The activities and organization of these 'invisible empires', which cut across national frontiers and may one day seriously curtail the economic initiatives of sovereign states, certainly form part of the history of post-war integration in Europe, even though they cannot be chronicled here. Other aspects of this 'informal' integration spring to mind: the motor car and the motorway have transformed Europe much as the railways did in the nineteenth century; a well-integrated European public opinion has emerged partly as a result of developments in television. Progress has been made even in intractable fields like sport and education. Once an English football team was fined by its professional organization for playing against a continental team; now, English clubs compete regularly for the European Cup (but not without displays of ill manners on the part of their supporters). In education, to give just one small example, progress has been made in the revision and 'de-nationalization' of history text-books; but space precludes the insertion in this book of the 1968 European Charter of Education; nor can we illustrate the activities of bodies like the Central Commission for Navigation on the Rhine, reputedly (in its various forms) the world's oldest international organization, nor those of international organizations like the European Conference of Ministers of Transport, Eurovision, or even Eurospace or the European Centre for Nuclear Research. All these and many more are contributing to the growing network of inter-state connections, to increasing international collaboration at all levels and in all fields. This process of what is, admittedly rather loosely, here called integration is certainly an important and diversified reality. Nonetheless, battered in the past by wars, and eroded now by these developments, the sovereign state lives on; nationalisms thrive; and it remains an open question whether or not, in Europe or elsewhere, some other political structure will emerge to replace the national sovereign state during what remains of the twentieth century.

I

Precursors

The four documents which make up this chapter illustrate the twofold nature of moves towards European integration, which have sometimes been governmental or public, sometimes private. All of them contain proposals for some kind of union or federation of existing states and they all date from before the close of the Second World War. The famous Memorandum (1) which has always gone under the name of its author Aristide Briand, then French Foreign Minister, was an official French government proposal. It embodied a series of suggestions put forward by M. Briand at Geneva on 9 September 1929 at the Tenth General Assembly of the League of Nations. This federal project represents the first official formulation of European integration ideas in a concrete political form. Our succinct excerpts perhaps mask an essential weakness of the Memorandum: it was too long and too vague. Nor was it received with much enthusiasm; most governments were reserved, England was hostile, and its complete abandonment was ensured by the Nazi electoral successes of 1930 and the death of its author in 1932. That other government-sponsored plan, the proposed Anglo-French Union of 1940 (2), was more visionary, more vague, more short-lived, and even more a product of international crisis. Significantly enough, three Frenchmen who were subsequently to play important roles in the history of European integration, helped to draft and produce it: General Charles de Gaulle, Jean Monnet and René Pleven. Churchill subscribed to it, more as a move to encourage the then Prime Minister of France, Paul Reynaud, to stay in the war against Germany, than as a seriously thought out, practical proposition.

On the island of Ventotene, some thirty miles off the eastern coast of Italy between Rome and Naples, a group of anti-fascist internees led by Altiero Spinelli, now a member of the European Commission, and Ernesto Rossi, drew up in July 1941 a plea for a European Federation (3) which was circulated clandestinely in Rome that very month. A year later it was printed in French at Toulouse. This plea drew its eventual inspiration in part from the writings of men like Carlo Sforza and

Luigi Einaudi and the pre-war Anglo-Saxon federalists; in part from the evident contemporary crisis of the nation state. Its authors founded the Movimento Federalista Europeo in Milan in August 1943 and then helped to bring together at Geneva an international group of federalists who published in July 1944 the first joint federalist declaration by activists from different countries (4). Their document was not just the dream of a few wise men; it probably represented the aspirations of many. A public opinion poll held in France a year later, on 15 July 1945, recorded that 75 per cent of those questioned were in favour of the recreation of Europe as a federation of states with 'all matters of common interest under the control of a democratically elected federal government'. As usual, however, it was the politicians, not the people, who had their way.

1   The Briand 'Memorandum on the organization of a regime of Federal Union in Europe', 1 May 1930

. . . Compelled by their geographical position to live together, the peoples of Europe, if they are to enjoy security and prosperity, must establish a permanent régime of joint responsibility for the rational organization of Europe.

There is no question of constituting a European group outside the League of Nations. On the contrary it is desired to bring the interests of Europe into harmony, under the control of the League, and in conformity with its spirit, by incorporating into its universal system a limited system which, by its very limitations, would be all the more effective. . . . Certain questions exist which are of particularly European interest and with regard to which the States of Europe may desire, in the interest of peace itself, to take separate action, more immediate and more direct than can be expected from the League. Such questions, moreover, they are specially competent to handle on account of their ethnical affinities and the common source of their civilization. It has happened more than once that the League itself, in the general exercise of its activities, has had to take into account the fact that Europe constitutes a geographical entity for the problems of which solutions may be discovered not suitable for application to the whole world. . . .

But even in cases specially reserved for the labours of the League of Nations the federal link between European States would be useful in preparing an atmosphere favourable to the pacific settlements of the League, or to the practical execution of its decisions. . . . For this reason the Representative of France has been concerned from the first to avoid all ambiguity, and, in taking the initiative of the first European meeting, he therefore took the view that it should consist only of representatives of those States which are members of the League of Nations and that it should be held in Geneva, concurrently with the Tenth Assembly; that is, in the atmosphere and within the framework of the League. . . .

The entente between European nations must be realized on the plane of their absolute sovereignty and complete political independence. Moreover, it would be impossible to associate the idea of political domination with any organization which (like the present one) is deliberately placed under the control of the League of Nations. . . .

By a formula, as comprehensive as possible, but clearly indicating the essential aim of the association, which is to serve the common cause of the organization of Europe for peace, the signatory Governments would bind themselves to maintain regular contact by meetings held periodically or specially convened meetings to examine together all questions of primary interest to the commonwealth of European peoples. . . .

. . . Never has the time been so propitious or so pressing for the beginning of constructive work in Europe. By the settlement of the principal moral and material problems arising out of the war Europe will soon be freed from heavy burdens, spiritual and economic. The new Europe will be ready for a positive effort, answering to the new order. It is the decisive hour for Europe to listen and choose her own fate. To unite, in order to live and prosper: that is the necessity which confronts European nations to-day. The peoples seem to have made their feelings clear: the Governments must now accept their responsibilities. Otherwise the grouping of material and moral forces for the common benefit which it is their collective task to control will be abandoned to the dangers and chances of uncoordinated individual initiatives.

The Times, 19 May 1930

2   Declaration of Anglo-French Union, 16 June 1940

At this most fateful moment in the history of the modern world the Governments of the United Kingdom and the French Republic make this declaration of indissoluble union and unyielding resolution in their common defence of justice and freedom against subjection to a system which reduces mankind to a life of robots and slaves.

The two Governments declare that France and Great Britain shall no longer be two nations, but one Franco-British Union.

The constitution of the Union will provide for joint organs of defence, foreign, financial, and economic policies.

Every citizen of France will enjoy immediately citizenship of Great Britain; every British subject will become a citizen of France.

Both countries will share responsibility for the repair of the devastation of war, wherever it occurs in their territories, and the resources of both shall be equally, and as one, applied to that purpose.

During the war there shall be a single War Cabinet, and all the forces of Britain and France, whether on land, sea, or in the air, will be placed under its direction. It will govern from wherever it best can. The two Parliaments will be formally associated. The nations of the British Empire are already forming new armies. France will keep her available forces in the field, on the sea, and in the air. The Union appeals to the United States to fortify the economic resources of the Allies, and to bring her powerful material aid to the common cause.

The Union will concentrate its whole energy against the power of the enemy, no matter where the battle may be.

And thus we shall conquer.

W. S. Churchill, *The Second World War*, 2. *Their finest hour*, 183–4. Cassell, 1949

3   The manifesto of Ventotene, July 1941

Every nation has an equal right to organize itself as an independent state. Every people, with its own ethnic, geographical, linguistic and historical characteristics, should be able to satisfy its needs in the best possible way, without interference from outside, by means of a governmental structure created according to its own particular approach to politics. The concept of national independence has been a powerful stimulus to progress: in response to foreign aggression it has replaced petty parochialism with a wider loyalty; it has swept away many of the obstacles which hampered the movement of goods and labour; it has provided the less advanced populations of each new state with the institutions and laws of more civilized peoples. But this concept carried within itself the seeds of capitalist imperialism which our generation has seen develop until it produced totalitarian states and unleashed the world wars.

Nowadays, the nation is no longer regarded as the historical by-product of a human community the members of which, thanks to a long process, have achieved sufficient unity in their habits and aspirations to discover in the state the best way of organising their way of life within the framework of mankind as a whole. Rather, the nation has become a divine entity which thinks only of its own existence and its own development, without caring at all about the damage it may cause to others. The absolute sovereignty of the nation states has caused each one of them to try to dominate the others, because each feels itself threatened by the power of the others. Moreover, each tries to extend its sphere of influence over an ever larger area, so as to allow itself freedom of action and to ensure for itself the means of subsistence without having to depend on others. The inevitable result of this desire to dominate is the hegemony of the strongest state over all the others, which are subjected to it. . . .

If in future the [revolutionary] struggle is still confined by the traditional national framework it will be extremely difficult to escape the old impasses. Indeed, the nation states have already planned their economies so thoroughly that the only important question will shortly be that of knowing which vested interest, or class, ought to be in control of the plan. Any united front of progressive forces could easily be shattered to pieces by these quarrels between classes and economic categories. Doubtless it will be the reactionaries who will benefit. . . .

The forces of reaction have men and leaders able and educated to command who will fight obstinately to maintain their supremacy. They will know how to disguise themselves in a crisis, proclaiming themselves lovers of liberty, of peace, of the general welfare, of the poorer classes. . . .

The fulcrum on which these elements will try to lever themselves into power will be the restoration of the nation state. They will thus be able to exploit that popular sentiment which is most widespread, most affected by recent events, most easily adaptable to reactionary aims; namely, the patriotic sentiment. This is the best way they can counter the ideas of their opponents, given that, so far, most people's only political experience has been within the national framework. Because of this, it will not be difficult to concentrate these somewhat myopic people on the task of reconstructing the states ruined by the catastrophe [of war].

If this aim is achieved the forces of reaction will have conquered. Even if these [reconstructed] states are democratic and socialist in appearance, the return to power of the reactionaries will merely be a matter of time. National jealousies will re-emerge and every state will once again think in terms of using force of arms to satisfy its particular demands. The main task will become that of converting peoples into armies as quickly as possible. The generals will return to their commands, the monopolists to profit from the need for self-sufficiency, the bureaucrats to feather their own nests, the priests to keep the people docile. All the initial achievements will shrivel to nothing because of the need for renewed military preparations.

The problem which must first be solved is the final abolition of the division of Europe into sovereign national states. Without this, any progress made will be appearance only. The crushing of most of the continental states under the German steam-roller has already given the European peoples a common destiny: either they will all remain subject to Hitler's rule or, with its collapse, they will together enter a revolutionary crisis in which they will no longer be constricted and separated by solid national structures. People are now much more in favour of a federal reorganization of Europe than they were in the past. The harsh experiences of the last ten years have opened the eyes even of those who had no wish to see; they have also brought about numerous circumstances favourable to our ideal.

Every thinking man now appreciates that it is impossible to maintain a balance of power among the independent European states so long as militarist Germany exists side by side with them. Nor will it be possible to reduce Germany to small pieces or hold it down after it has been defeated. In proof of this, it has become clear that no European country can remain apart while the others wage war; declarations of neutrality and pacts of non-aggression have become valueless. The futility, even the harmfulness, of institutions like the League of Nations, has been demonstrated; they pretend to guarantee international law, but without the military force needed to enforce their decisions, and they respect the absolute sovereignty of their member states. The principle of non-intervention, according to which every population is free to give itself whatever kind of despotic government it thinks best, has proved absurd; as if the internal constitution of every single state is not a vital interest for all the other European countries. The manifold problems which bedevil the international affairs of the continent have become insoluble: definition of the boundaries in areas of mixed populations, protection of rights of ethnic minorities, outlets to the sea for inland countries, Balkan question, Irish question, etc. All of them could most easily be resolved by a European Federation. Historically, similar problems arising between the petty principalities which went to make up the larger national unities lost their bitterness on being transformed into relations between one province and another.

On the other hand, the disappearance of the sense of security which had resulted from the impregnability of Great Britain, and which had brought about the 'splendid isolation' of the English, the collapse of the French army and the Republic of France itself at the first serious onslaught of the German forces, . . . and, above all, awareness of the serious danger of universal subjection, all are circumstances favouring the establishment of a federal regime which would bring today's anarchy to an end. And the fact that England has now accepted the principle of Indian independence, and France by acknowledging her defeat has potentially lost her empire, will make it easier to find some basis of agreement for a 'European' administration of former colonial possessions.

Finally, to all this one must add the disappearance of some of the principal dynasties and the weakness of the foundations on which those surviving rest. For it must be appreciated that these dynasties, which regard the various countries as their traditional apanages, together with the powerful interests they supported, have constituted a serious obstacle to the rational organization of the United States of Europe, which can only be based on a republican constitution comprising all the federated countries. And when, conquering the horizons of the old continent, all the peoples of the world embrace each other in a vision of unity, we need to recognize that the European Federation is the only conceivable guarantee that relations with the Asiatic and American peoples can be based on pacific cooperation, until a more distant future when the political unity of the entire globe becomes possible. . . .

Comunita europee, Dec. 1973, 32–9; editor's
translation approved by Signor Spinelli

4 Draft declaration of the European Resistance Movements July 1944

Activists from the Resistance Movements of Denmark, France, Italy, Norway, the Netherlands, Poland, Czechoslovakia and Yugoslavia and the Representative of an active anti-Nazi group in Germany met in a city in Europe on 31 March, 29 April, 20 May and 6 and 7 July 1944. They drafted the following Declaration which is herewith submitted for discussion and approval by their respective Movements and by the whole of the Resistance Movements of Europe. They believe that they should immediately transmit their draft to international public opinion but reserve their right to publish it in its final form when it has been accepted by the Movements, groups and parties to which it is submitted.

I

Resistance to Naxi oppression, which unites the people of Europe in the same battle, has created among them a solidarity and a community of aim and of interest whose significance and meaning is expressed in the fact that delegates from the Resistance Movements of Europe have met to set out this Declaration in which they wish to express their hopes and their intentions for the fate of civilization and of peace.

The free men who take part today in resistance movements are aware that the incessant fight which they are conducting in spite of all terror on the front of internal resistance against the war machine of the enemy is an important positive contribution to the battle being fought by the United Nations and that it gives their countries the right to take part in the building of peace and of the reconstruction of Europe on the same basis as the other victorious powers.

Subscribing to the central declarations of the Atlantic Charter, they reaffirm that the life of the peoples which they represent must be based on the respect of the human individual, on security, on social justice, on the complete utilization of economic resources for the benefit of the whole and on the autonomous development of national life.

II

These aims cannot be fulfilled unless the different countries of the world agree to go beyond the dogma of the absolute sovereignty of the state and unite in a single federal organization.

The lack of unity and cohesion that still exists between the different parts of the world will not allow us to achieve immediately an organization that unites all civilizations under a single federal government. At the end of this war one will therefore have to be content with setting up a universal organization of a less ambitious kind, but one able to develop in the direction of federal unity, in which the great civilizations on which it rests will pursue the task of ensuring collective security. But this cannot be an efficient instrument of peace unless the great civilizations are organized in such a fashion that the spirit of peace and of understanding can prevail.

That is why within the framework of this universal organization the European problem must be given a more direct and a more radical solution.

III

The peace of Europe is the cornerstone of world peace. Within a single generation Europe has now been the focal centre of two world conflicts which were due above all to the existence on this continent of thirty sovereign states. This anarchy must be remedied by the creation of a Federal Union between the European peoples.

Only a Federal Union will allow the German people to participate in the life of Europe without being a danger for the rest.

Only a Federal Union will allow the problems of frontier demarcation in areas of mixed population to be resolved—problems which will thus cease to be the object of stupid nationalist covetousness and will become simple questions of the territorial demarcation of purely administrative powers.

Only a Federal Union will allow democratic institutions to be safeguarded in such a way that countries that are insufficiently mature politically cannot endanger the general order.

Only a Federal Union will allow the economic reconstruction of the continent and the elimination of monopolies and national autarchies.

Only a Federal Union will allow a logical and natural solution to the problems of access to the sea for landlocked countries, the rational utilization of the rivers that run through more than one state, the control of straits and generally most of those problems that have upset international relations in recent years.

IV

One cannot now foresee the geographical limits of the Federal Union that will ensure the peace of Europe. But it must be sufficiently strong and sufficiently large for there to be no risk of it becoming the sphere of influence of a foreign state or the instrument of a hegemonial policy by one of its members. Moreover it must from the beginning be open to all countries that belong either wholly or partly to Europe and which can and wish to become members of it. The Federal Union must be based on a declaration of civil, political and economic rights which guarantees the free development of the human personality and the normal functioning of democratic institutions; moreover it must rest on a declaration of the rights of minorities to an autonomous existence compatible with the integrity of the nation states of which they form a part.

The Federal Union must not prejudice the right of each of the member countries to solve its own special problems according to its own ethnic and cultural characteristics. But given the experiences and the failures of the League of Nations, the member states must irrevocably surrender to the Federation those aspects of their sovereignty that deal with the defence of their territory, relations with states outside the Federal Union, and international trade and communications.

The Federal Union must essentially have (i) a government responsible not to the governments of the various member states but to their peoples, over which it must be able to exercise direct jurisdiction within the limits of its powers; (ii) an army placed under the orders of this government and excluding all other national armies; (iii) a supreme tribunal which will judge all questions as to the interpretation of the federal constitution and which will settle any differences there may be between member states or between the states and the federation.

V

The peace to be born out of this war must be founded on justice and progress and not on revenge and reaction. It must show itself implacable against all war criminals, whose impunity would be an insult to the sacrifice made by the war dead and particularly the anonymous heroes of the European Resistance. Germany and its satellites must take part in the economic reconstruction of the regions they have devastated, but Germany must be helped and if necessary forced to transform her own political and economic structure so that she can take her place in the Federal Union. For that she must be totally disarmed and temporarily subjected to a federal control which shall have as its principal tasks:

To entrust power to those sincerely democratic elements that have fought an unequivocal battle against Nazism;

To reconstruct a decentralized and democratic state where there will be no trace left of Prussian bureaucracy and militarism;

To demand the radical destruction of the feudal system of agriculture and of industry;

To integrate the heavy and chemical industry of Germany into European industrial organization so that it can no longer be used for German nationalist aims;

To ensure that the education of German youth does not follow Nazi, militarist or totalitarian doctrines.

VI

The undersigned movements of resistance recognize the need for an active participation of the United Nations in the solution of the European problem, but demand that all the measures that are taken between the end of hostilities and the establishment of peace are taken with a view to the needs of the federal organization.

They appeal to all the spiritual and political forces of the world and particularly to those of the United Nations for help in achieving the aims set out in this Declaration.

They undertake to consider their respective national problems as special aspects of the European problem as a whole, and they decide to set up immediately a permanent office to coordinate their efforts for the liberation of their countries, for the organization of the Federal Union of the European peoples, and to build peace and justice in the world.

U. Kitzinger, *The European Common Market and Community*, 29–33. London, 1967

II

First steps in the West, 1947–1949

The first and last documents in this group illustrate the overriding importance of the American contribution to the first post-war efforts at integration in Europe. Churchill's speech at Zürich University in 1946, in which he called for a 'Council of Europe' to be the first step in the creation of 'a regional structure called, it may be, the United States of Europe,' has often been regarded as a sort of foundation stone of post-war European integration. But the real foundations for European recovery and all that went with it, including the eventual formation of the Common Market, were laid by American Secretary of State General George C. Marshall in a speech at Harvard University on 5 June 1947, when he received the honorary degree of Doctor of Laws (5). On that occasion the financial assistance that came to be called Marshall Aid was inaugurated. The transference of these funds to Europe, and their distribution there, were accompanied by consistent pressure from the United States in favour of cooperation and integration between the West European states. For example, the report of Paul G. Hoffman's speech to the Council of the OEEC in Paris on 31 October (12) was printed in the *New York Times*, next to a statement that: 'The Truman Administration has no intention of asking Congress for a third Marshall Plan appropriation unless Western European governments can agree by January on a plan of European integration that cuts across present state boundaries. . . .'

Of course, the European powers did not agree on so radical a programme; but they had in fact already made some progress, in cooperation if not integration. In the spring of 1948 the Convention for European Economic Cooperation (7) had established the OEEC to administer the Marshall Aid funds and promote economic cooperation, and the Hague Congress (8) had firmly demonstrated the continuing existence of a substantial body of federalist opinion in Europe. Early in 1949 the International Council of the newly formed European Movement held its first meeting (9) and followed this up with the Westminster Economic Conference in April 1949, the aim of which was to discuss the measures needed to achieve 'European Economic Union' and the 'general principles to be followed in any international integration of basic industries and agriculture'. By the summer of 1949 the Council of Europe was already established (11); the first meeting of its Consultative Assembly opened on 10 August of that year at Strasbourg in a mood of federal enthusiasm and with high hopes for the future of European unity.

Meanwhile, in response to the step-by-step extension of Soviet power in Eastern Europe in 1947 which culminated in the formation of a communist government in Czechoslovakia in February 1948, and as a result of increasing fears of Soviet nationalism and military ambition, the West European powers began to consider the desirability of allying together for their collective defence. The Treaty of Dunkirk had been signed by Britain and France on 4 March 1947 specifically against possible German aggression; a year later, on 17 March 1948, Belgium, Luxembourg and the Netherlands persuaded these two powers to sign the Treaty of Brussels (6) which was later (1954) transformed by means of the inclusion of the German Federal Republic and Italy, into the Western European Union. NATO (10), which was set up a year after the Brussels Treaty Organization, went further, because it included the United States and Canada in a single defence system together with the Brussels Treaty signatories and Denmark, Norway, Iceland, Italy and Portugal. Although NATO is intergovernmental rather than supranational in character it does embody a measure of real integration, both in the staffs at the different NATO headquarters, in exercises, and in certain permanent air and naval units.

5 Speech of Secretary of State George Marshall at Harvard University, 5 June 1947

I need not tell you gentlemen that the world situation is very serious. That must be apparent to all intelligent people. I think one difficulty is that the problem is one of such enormous complexity that the very mass of facts presented to the public by press and radio make it exceedingly difficult for the man in the street to reach a clear appraisement of the situation. Futhermore, the people of this country are distant from the troubled areas of the earth and it is hard for them to comprehend the plight and consequent reactions of the long-suffering peoples, and the effect of those reactions on their governments in connection with our efforts to promote peace in the world.

In considering the requirements for the rehabilitation of Europe, the physical loss of life, the visible destruction of cities, factories, mines, and railroads was correctly estimated, but it has become obvious during recent months that this visible destruction was probably less serious than the dislocation of the entire fabric of European economy. For the past ten years conditions have been highly abnormal. The feverish preparation for war and the more feverish maintenance of the war effort engulfed all aspects of national economies. Machinery has fallen into disrepair or is entirely obsolete. Under the arbitrary and destructive Nazi rule, virtually every possible enterprise was geared into the German war machine. Long-standing commercial ties, private institutions, banks, insurance companies, and shipping companies disappeared, through loss of capital, absorption through nationalization, or by simple destruction. In many countries, confidence in the local currency has been severely shaken. The breakdown of the business structure of Europe during the war was complete. Recovery has been seriously retarded by the fact that two years after the close of hostilities a peace settlement with Germany and Austria has not been agreed upon. But even given a more prompt solution of these difficult problems, the rehabilitation of the economic structure of Europe quite evidently will require a much longer time and greater effort than had been foreseen. . . . The truth of the matter is that Europe's requirements for the next three or four years of foreign food and other essential products—principally from America—are so much greater than her present ability to pay that she must have substantial additional help or face economic, social, and political deterioration of a very grave character.

The remedy lies in breaking the vicious circle and restoring the confidence of the European people in the economic future of their own countries and of Europe as a whole. The manufacturer and the farmer throughout wide areas must be able and willing to exchange their products for currencies the continuing value of which is not open to question.

Aside from the demoralizing effect on the world at large and the possibilities of disturbances arising as a result of the desperation of the people concerned, the consequences to the economy of the United States should be apparent to all. It is logical that the United States should do whatever it is able to do to assist in the return of normal economic health in the world, without which there can be no political stability and no assured peace. Our policy is directed not against any country or doctrine but against hunger, poverty, desperation, and chaos. Its purpose should be the revival of a working economy in the world so as to permit the emergence of political and social conditions in which free institutions can exist. Such assistance, I am convinced, must not be on a piecemal basis as various crises develop. Any assistance that this Government may render in the future should provide a cure rather than a mere palliative. Any government that is willing to assist in the task of recovery will find full cooperation, I am sure, on the part of the United States Government. Any government which manœuvres to block the recovery of other countries cannot expect help from us. Furthermore, governments, political parties, or groups which seek to perpetuate human misery in order to profit therefrom politically or otherwise will encounter the opposition of the United States.

It is already evident that, before the United States Government can proceed much further in its efforts to alleviate the situation and help start the European world on its way to recovery, there must be some agreement among the countries of Europe as to the requirements of the situation and the part those countries themselves will take in order to give proper effect to whatever action might be undertaken by this Government. It would be neither fitting nor efficacious for this Government to undertake to draw up unilaterally a programme designed to place Europe on its feet economically. This is the business of the Europeans. The initiative, I think, must come from Europe. The role of this country should consist of friendly aid in the drafting of a European programme and of later support of such a programme so far as it may be practical for us to do so. The programme should be a joint one, agreed to by a number, if not all, European nations. . . .

Department of State Bulletin, 15 June 1947

6 Treaty of Economic, Social and Cultural Collaboration and Collective Self-defence, signed at Brussels, 17 March 1948, with the 1954 Protocol

His Royal Highness the Prince Regent of Belgium, the President of the French Republic, President of the French Union, Her Royal Highness the Grand Duchess of Luxembourg, Her Majesty the Queen of the Netherlands and His Majesty the King of Great Britain, Ireland and the British Dominions beyond the Seas,

Resolved

To reaffirm their faith in fundamental human rights, in the dignity and worth of the human person and in the other ideals proclaimed in the Charter of the United Nations;

To fortify and preserve the principles of democracy, personal freedom and political liberty, the constitutional traditions and the rule of law, which are their common heritage;

To strengthen, with these aims in view, the economic, social and cultural ties by which they are already united;

To cooperate loyally and to coordinate their efforts to create in Western Europe a firm basis for European economic recovery;

To afford assistance to each other, in accordance with the Charter of the United Nations, in maintaining international peace and security and in resisting any policy of aggression;

To take such steps as may be held to be necessary in the event of a renewal by Germany of a policy of aggression;

To associate progressively in the pursuance of these aims other states inspired by the same ideals and animated by the like determination;

Desiring for these purposes to conclude a treaty for collaboration in economic, social and cultural matters and for collective self-defence;

Have appointed as their Plenipotentiaries:

(*Here follow the names of the plenipotentiaries*)

Who, having exhibited their full powers found in good and due form, have agreed as follows:

Article 1

Convinced of the close community of their interests and of the necessity of uniting in order to promote the economic recovery of Europe, the High Contracting Parties will so organize and coordinate their economic activities as to produce the best possible results, by the elimination of conflict in their economic policies, the coordination of production and the development of commercial exchanges.

The cooperation provided for in the preceding paragraph, which will be effected through the Consultative Council referred to in Article 7 as well as through other bodies, shall not involve any duplication of, or prejudice to, the work of other economic organizations in which the High Contracting Parties are or may be represented but shall on the contrary assist the work of those organizations.

Article 2

The High Contracting Parties will make every effort in common, both by direct consultation and in specialized agencies, to promote the attainment of a higher standard of living by their peoples and to develop on corresponding lines the social and other related services of their countries.

The High Contracting Parties will consult with the object of achieving the earliest possible application of recommendations of immediate practical interest, relating to social matters, adopted with their approval in the specialized agencies.

They will endeavour to conclude as soon as possible conventions with each other in the sphere of social security.

Article 3

The High Contracting Parties will make every effort in common to lead their peoples towards a better understanding of the principles which form the basis of their common civilization and to promote cultural exchanges by conventions between themselves or by other means.

Article 4

If any of the High Contracting Parties should be the object of an armed attack in Europe, the other High Contracting Parties will, in accordance with the provisions of Article 51 of the Charter of the United Nations, afford the Party so attacked all the military and other aid and assistance in their power.

Article 5

All measures taken as a result of the preceding Article shall be immediately reported to the Security Council. They shall be terminated as soon as the Security Council has taken the measures necessary to maintain or restore international peace and security.

The present Treaty does not prejudice in any way the obligations of the High Contracting Parties under the provisions of the Charter of the United Nations. It shall not be interpreted as affecting in any way the authority and responsibility of the Security Council under the Charter to take at any time such action as it deems necessary in order to maintain or restore international peace and security. . . .

Article 7

For the purpose of consulting together on all the questions dealt with in the present Treaty, the High Contracting Parties will create a Consultative Council, which shall be so organized as to be able to exercise its functions continuously. The Council shall meet at such times as it shall deem fit.

At the request of any of the High Contracting Parties, the Council shall be immediately convened in order to permit the High Contracting Parties to consult with regard to any situation which may constitute a threat to peace, in whatever area this threat should arise; with regard to the attitude to be adopted and the steps to be taken in case of a renewal by Germany of an aggressive policy; or with regard to any situation constituting a danger to economic stability. . . .

Article 10

The present Treaty shall be ratified and the instruments of ratification shall be deposited as soon as possible with the Belgian Government.

It shall enter into force on the date of the deposit of the last instrument of ratification and shall thereafter remain in force for fifty years.

After the expiry of the period of fifty years, each of the High Contracting Parties shall have the right to cease to be a party thereto provided that he shall have previously given one year's notice of denunciation to the Belgian Government.

The Belgian Government shall inform the Governments of the other High Contracting Parties of the deposit of each instrument of ratification and of each notice of denunciation.

In witness whereof, the above-mentioned Plenipotentiaries have signed the present Treaty and have affixed thereto their seals.

Done at Brussels, this seventeenth day of March 1948, in English and French, each text being equally authentic, in a single copy which shall remain deposited in the archives of the Belgian Government and of which certified copies shall be transmitted by the Government to each of the other signatories.

Cmd. 7367. London, HMSO

Protocol, modifying and completing the Brussels Treaty, signed at
Paris on 23 October 1954

The High Contracting Parties to the Treaty of Economic, Social and
Cultural Collaboration and Collective Self-Defence, signed at Brussels
on March 17 1948, hereinafter referred to as the Treaty, on the one
hand,

and the President of the Federal Republic of Germany and the
President of the Italian Republic on the other hand,

Inspired by a common will to strengthen peace and security;

Desirous to this end of promoting the unity and of encouraging the
progressive integration of Europe;

Convinced that the accession of the Federal Republic of Germany
and the Italian Republic to the Treaty will represent a new and
substantial advance towards these aims:

Having taken into consideration the decisions of the London
Conference as set out in the Final Act of 3 October 1954, and its
Annexes;

(*Here follow the names of the Plenipotentiaries*)

Have agreed as follows:

Article 1

The Federal Republic of Germany and the Italian Republic hereby
accede to the Treaty as modified and completed by the present
Protocol.

The High Contracting Parties to the present Protocol consider the
Protocol on Forces of Western European Union (hereinafter referred
to as Protocol No. II), the Protocol on the Control of Armaments and
its Annexes (hereinafter referred to as Protocol No. III), and the
Protocol on the Agency of Western European Union for the Control of
Armaments (hereinafter referred to as Protocol No. IV) to be an
integral part of the present Protocol.

Article 2

The sub-paragraph of the Preamble to the Treaty: 'to take such
steps as may be held necessary in the event of renewal by Germany of a
policy of aggression' shall be modified to read: 'to promote the unity
and to encourage the progressive integration of Europe.'

The opening words of the second paragraph of Article 1 shall read:
'The cooperation provided for in the preceding paragraph, which will
be effected through the Council referred to in Article 8. . . .'

Article 3

The following new Article shall be inserted in the Treaty as Article 4: 'In the execution of the Treaty the High Contracting Parties and any organs established by Them under the Treaty shall work in close cooperation with the North Atlantic Treaty Organization.

'Recognizing the undesirability of duplicating the Military Staffs of NATO, the Council and its agency will rely on the appropriate Military Authorities of NATO for information and advice on military matters.'

Articles 4, 5, 6 and 7 of the Treaty will become respectively Articles 5, 6, 7 and 8.

Article 4

Article 8 of the Treaty (formerly Article 7) shall be modified to read as follows:

'1. For the purposes of strengthening peace and security and of promoting unity and of encouraging the progressive integration of Europe and closer cooperation between Them and with other European organizations, the High Contracting Parties to the Brussels Treaty shall create a Council to consider matters concerning the execution of this Treaty and of its Protocols and their Annexes.

'2. This Council shall be known as the 'Council of Western European Union'; it shall be so organized as to be able to exercise its functions continuously; it shall set up such subsidiary bodies as may be considered necessary; in particular it shall establish immediately an Agency for the Control of Armaments whose functions are defined in Protocol No. IV.

'3. At the request of any of the High Contracting Parties the Council shall be immediately convened in order to permit Them to consult with regard to any situation which may constitute a threat to peace, in whatever area this threat should arise, or a danger to economic stability.

'4. The Council shall decide by unanimous vote questions for which no other voting procedure has been or may be agreed. In the cases provided for in Protocols II, III and IV it will follow the various voting procedures, unanimity, two thirds majority, simple majority, laid down therein. It will decide by simple majority questions submitted to it by the Agency for the Control of Armaments.'

Article 5

A new Article shall be inserted in the Treaty as Article 9: 'The Council of Western European Union shall make an Annual Report on its activities and in particular concerning the control of armaments to an Assembly composed of representatives of the Brussels Treaty Powers to the Consultative Assembly of the Council of Europe.'

The Articles 8, 9 and 10 of the Treaty shall become respectively Articles 10, 11 and 12.

Article 6

The present Protocol and the other Protocols listed in Article 1 above shall be ratified and the instruments of ratification shall be deposited as soon as possible with the Belgian Government. . . .

In witness whereof the above-mentioned Plenipotentiaries have signed the present Protocol and have affixed thereto their seals.

Done at Paris this twenty-third day of October, 1954, in two texts, in the English and French languages, each text being equally authoritative, in a single copy which shall remain deposited in the archives of the Belgian Government and of which certified copies shall be transmitted by that Government to each of the other signatories.

Text supplied by the Secretariat-General of WEU

7 Convention for European Economic Cooperation, Paris, 16 April 1948

The Governments of Austria, Belgium, Denmark, France, Greece, Ireland, Iceland, Italy, Luxembourg, Norway, the Netherlands, Portugal, the United Kingdom, Sweden, Switzerland and Turkey, and the Commanders-in-Chief of the French, United Kingdom and United States Zones of Occupation of Germany:

Considering that a strong and prosperous European economy is essential for the attainment of the purpose of the United Nations, the preservation of individual liberty and the increase of general well-being, and that it will contribute to the maintenance of peace;

Recognizing that their economic systems are interrelated and that the prosperity of each of them depends on the prosperity of all;

Believing that only by close and lasting cooperation between the Contracting Parties can the prosperity of Europe be restored and maintained, and the ravages of war made good;

Resolved to implement the principles and to achieve the aims set forth in the General Report of the Committee of European Economic Cooperation, particularly the speedy establishment of sound economic conditions enabling the Contracting Parties as soon as possible to achieve and maintain a satisfactory level of economic activity without extraordinary outside assistance, and to make their full contribution to world economic stability;

Determined to combine their economic strength to these ends, to join together to make the fullest collective use of their individual capacities and potentialities, to increase their production, develop and modernize their industrial and agricultural equipment, expand their commerce, reduce progressively barriers to trade among themselves, promote full employment and restore or maintain the stability of their economies and general confidence in their national currencies;

Taking note of the generous resolve of the American people expressed in the action taken to furnish the assistance without which the aims set forth above cannot be fully achieved;

Resolved to create the conditions and establish the institutions necessary for the success of European economic cooperation and for the effective use of American aid, and to conclude a Convention to this end;

Have accordingly appointed the undersigned Plenipotentiaries who, having presented their full powers, found in good and due form, have agreed on the following provisions:

Article 1

The Contracting Parties agree to work in close cooperation in their economic relations with one another.

As their immediate task, they will undertake the elaboration and execution of a joint recovery programme. The object of this programme will be to achieve as soon as possible and maintain a satisfactory level of economic activity without extraordinary outside assistance, and to this end the programme will take special account of the need of the Contracting Parties to develop their exports to non-participating countries to the maximum extent possible.

Accordingly the Contracting Parties pledge themselves to carry out, by their efforts of self-help and in a spirit of mutual aid, the following General Obligations, and hereby set up an Organization for European Economic Cooperation, hereinafter referred to as the Organization.

PART I: GENERAL OBLIGATIONS
Article 2

The Contracting Parties will, both individually and collectively, promote with vigour the development of production, through efficient use of the resources at their command, whether in their metropolitan or overseas territories, and by the progressive modernization of equipment and techniques, in such manner as may best assist the accomplishment of the joint recovery programme.

Article 3

The Contracting Parties will, within the framework of the Organization and as often and to such extent as may be necessary, draw up general programmes for the production and exchange of commodities and services. In so doing they will take into consideration their several estimates or programmes and general world economic conditions.

Each Contracting Party will use its best endeavours to secure the fulfilment of such general programmes.

Article 4

The Contracting Parties will develop, in mutual cooperation, the maximum possible interchange of goods and services. To this end they will continue the efforts already initiated to achieve as soon as possible a multilateral system of payments among themselves, and will cooperate in relaxing restrictions on trade and payments between one another, with the object of abolishing as soon as possible those restrictions which at present hamper such trade and payments.

In the application of this Article, the Contracting Parties will take due account of the necessity that they should, collectively and individually, correct or avoid excessive disequilibrium in their financial and economic relations, both amongst themselves and with non-participating countries.

Article 5

The Contracting Parties agree to strengthen their economic links by all methods which they may determine will further the objectives of the present Convention. They will continue the study of Customs Unions or analogous arrangements such as free trade areas, the formation of which might constitute one of the methods of achieving these objectives. Those Contracting Parties which have already agreed in principle to the creation of Customs Unions will further the establishment of such Unions as rapidly as conditions permit.

Article 6

The Contracting Parties will cooperate with one another and with other like-minded countries in reducing tariff and other barriers to the expansion of trade, with a view to achieving a sound and balanced multilateral trading system such as will accord with the principles of the Havana Charter.[1]

Article 7

Each Contracting Party will, having due regard to the need for a high and stable level of trade and employment and for avoiding or countering the dangers of inflation, take such steps as lie within its power to achieve or maintain the stability of its currency and of its internal financial position, sound rates of exchange and, generally, confidence in its monetary system.

Article 8

The Contracting Parties will make the fullest and most effective use of their available man-power.

They will endeavour to provide full employment for their own people and they may have recourse to man-power available in the territory of any other Contracting Party. In the latter case they will, in mutual agreement, take the necessary measures to facilitate the movement of workers and to ensure their establishment in conditions satisfactory from the economic and social point of view.

Generally, the Contracting Parties will cooperate in the progressive reduction of obstacles to the free movement of persons.

Article 9

The Contracting Parties will furnish the Organization with all the information it may request of them in order to facilitate the accomplishment of its tasks.

PART II: THE ORGANIZATION

Article 10: Membership

The Members of the Organization shall be the Parties to the present Convention.

Article 11: Aim

The aim of the Organization shall be the achievement of a sound European economy through the economic cooperation of its

---

[1] A Charter incorporating universal rules for the conduct of commerce, drawn up at an international economic conference in the winter of 1947–8 but never ratified.

members. An immediate task of the Organization will be to ensure the success of the European recovery programme, in accordance with the undertakings contained in Part I of the present Convention.

Article 12: Functions

Within the limits of such powers as are or may be agreed for the Organization, its functions shall be.

(a) to prepare and implement, within the sphere of the collective action of the Members concerned, the measures necessary to achieve the aim laid down in Article 11 and to facilitate, promote and coordinate the individual action of the Members;

(b) to facilitate and review the implementation of the present Convention; to take such action as may be found appropriate in order to ensure its execution; and to this end, to provide for systems of observation and review adequate to ensure the efficient use both of external aid and of indigenous resources;

(c) to provide the United States Government with such assistance and information as may be agreed in relation to the execution of the European recovery programme and to address recommendations to that Government;

(d) at the request of the interested parties, to assist in the negotiation of such international agreements as may be necessary for the better execution of the European recovery programme.

The Organization may also assume such other functions as may be agreed.

Article 13: Powers

In order to achieve its aim as set out in Article 11 the Organization may:

(a) take decisions for implementation by Members;

(b) enter into agreements with its Members, non-member countries, the United States Government and International Organizations;

(c) make recommendations to the United States Government, to other Governments, and to International Organizations.

Article 14: Decisions

Unless the Organization otherwise agrees for special cases, decisions shall be taken by mutual agreement of all the Members. The abstention of any Members declaring themselves not to be interested in the subject under discussion shall not invalidate decisions, which shall be binding for the other Members.

Article 15: The Council

(a) A Council composed of all the Members shall be the body from which all decisions derive.

(b) The Council shall designate annually from among the Members a Chairman and two Vice-Chairmen.

(c) The Council shall be assisted by an Executive Committee and a Secretary-General. The Council may set up such technical committees or other bodies as may be required for the performance of the functions of the Organization. All such organs shall be responsible to the Council. . . .

Cmd. 7388. London, HMSO

8 Resolution of the Political Committee of the Congress of Europe at The Hague, May 1948

The ravages wrought by six years of war and by the [German] occupation, the diminution of world food production, the destruction of industrial capacity, the creation of huge debts, the maintenance of military expenditure out of all proportion to the resources of the people, the shifting of economic power, the rancours left by war, the progressive evils of nationalism and the absence, despite the work of UNO, of an international authority sufficiently strong to provide law and order, constitute an unprecedented menace to the well-being and the security of the peoples of Europe and threaten them with ruin.

In accordance with the principles and objectives set out in the Political Report submitted by the International Committee of the Movements for European Unity:

The Congress:

1. Recognizes that it is the urgent duty of the nations of Europe to create an economic and political union in order to assure security and social progress;

2. Notes with approval the recent steps which have been taken by some European Governments in the direction of economic and political cooperation, but believes that in the present emergency the organizations created are by themselves insufficient to provide any lasting remedy;

3. Declares that the time has come when the European nations must transfer and merge some portion of their sovereign rights so as to secure common political and economic action for the integration and proper development of their common resources;

4. Demands the convening, as a matter of real urgency, of a European Assembly chosen by the Parliaments of the participating nations, from among their members and others, designed

—to stimulate and give expression to European public opinion;

—to advise upon immediate practical measures designed progressively to bring about the necessary economic and political union of Europe;

—to examine the juridical and constitutional implications arising out of the creation of such a Union or Federation and their economic and social consequences;

—to prepare the necessary plans for the above purposes;

5. Considers that the resultant Union or Federation should be open to all European nations democratically governed and which undertake to respect a Charter of Human Rights;

Resolves that a Commission should be set up to undertake immediately the double task of drafting such a Charter and of laying down standards to which a State must conform if it is to deserve the name of a democracy;

—Declares that in no circumstances shall a State be entitled to be called a democracy unless it does, in fact as well has in law, guarantee to its citizens liberty of thought, assembly and expression, as well as the right to form a political opposition;

Requests that this Commission should report within three months on its labours;

6. Is convinced that in the interests of human values and human liberty, the Assembly should make proposals for the establishment of a Court of Justice with adequate sanctions for the implementation of this Charter, and to this end any citizen of the associated countries shall have redress before the court, at any time and with the least possible delay, of any violation of his rights as formulated in the Charter;

7. Affirms that the integration of Germany in a United or Federated Europe alone provides a solution to both the economic and political aspects of the German problem;

8. Considers that any Union or Federation of Europe should be designed to protect the security of its constituent peoples, should be free from outside control, and should not be directed against any other nation;

9. Assigns to a United Europe the immediate task of establishing progressively a democratic social system, the aim of which shall be to free men from all types of slavery and economic insecurity, just as

political democracy aims at protecting them against the exercise of arbitrary power;

10. Declares that the Union or Federation must assist in assuring the economic, political and cultural advancement of the populations of the overseas territories associated with it, without prejudice to the special ties which now link these territories to European countries;

11. Declares that the creation of a United Europe is an essential element in the creation of a united world.

Landmarks in European Unity, 37–41. Ed. S.
Patijn, Sijthoff, Leyden

9 Declaration of Political Principles of European Union approved by the International Council of the European Movement at Brussels, 28 February 1949

1. In a world dominated by political and economic units of continental dimensions, the European nations cannot hope to survive on a basis of political or economic independence. Europe must unite, not merely to preserve the peace and freedom of her peoples and to recover and augment her material prosperity, but to assert once more those principles which are now menaced and which must be preserved and given new life by being enshrined in a new structure.

2. Love of freedom, hostility to totalitarianism of every kind, the humble and conscientious search for truth and, above all, respect for the human personality and for the individual as an individual—these are the essential characteristics of the true spirit of Europe. From them there springs, not a grudging toleration of diversity, but a glad recognition of its merit. These moral values, which are the product of two thousand years of civilization and were reaffirmed in the resistance to Nazism and Fascism, must inspire the organization of Europe.

3. European culture is expressed through that tradition of democracy which is shared by all our nations. All of us believe in a rule of law which is independent of the State, and which at the same time provides the foundations and fixes the limits of State authority. We believe that the human personality is sacrosanct and that the fundamental liberties attaching to it must be guaranteed against all forms of tyranny. We further believe that the individual exists only in relation to his fellows and as a member of organic communities. Such communities must, within the limits of their competence, enjoy a considerable degree of autonomy, provided always that the necessary collective discipline is maintained. Finally, we believe that the concept

of democracy implies freedom of criticism and therefore the right of opposition.

4. A political institution or an economic and social system is never an end in itself; it is merely a means of creating favourable conditions in which the human personality can develop and expand. Economic power should be regarded as a responsibility to be discharged in the best interests of all. The methods employed, as well as the political and economic institutions to be created, must, above all, inspire a sense of personal responsibility and must encourage individual initiative to the maximum.

5. Europe is being born at a time when its constituent nations are undergoing a profound social transformation. Within the new organisms the workers must play their part in management and in the exercise of authority to the full extent of their technical and political capacity.

6. It is not a question of choosing between liberty and authority, nor between a free and a collective economy, but of creating a synthesis of the two, which, far from being in opposition to one another, can be combined for constructive purposes.

7. No State should be admitted into the European Union which does not accept the fundamental principles of a Charter of Human Rights, and which does not declare itself willing and bound to ensure their application. In consequence, the official adherence of certain European nations, both in the West and in the East, cannot be counted upon for the present. But the barrier which divides the free States from the other European nations must not be accepted as permanent. Our aim is the union in freedom of all the peoples of Europe.

8. Western Germany must be invited forthwith (and the rest of Germany when possible) to become an integral part of this new community, in which the citizens of all the nations will have the same rights and the same duties.

9. Any Union must take account of the special ties which unite certain nations with countries overseas. The traditional links between European States and other self-governing countries overseas must be preserved and extended for the mutual benefit of all. Europe must also actively help territories which are now dependent to evolve towards a regime of autonomy. They must be permitted to participate fully in the political, economic and social benefits of the European association, and to be represented in European organizations according to the constitutional practices in each country.

10. European values can only be preserved in so far as they are given

new life and substance through the medium of new political institutions. In the absence of such new institutions, the European organizations and services, which are already in being or in process of being created, will rapidly become ineffective, or will be driven by force of circumstances to usurp the functions of government by setting up in their place an uncontrolled technocracy.

11. There are, thus, both moral and material considerations which demand the union of Europe. The tolerance of diversity, which has enabled her to play so noble a part in history, will find expression in a new order in which liberty joins hands with discipline. From this there will flow a fresh inspiration, which will assure to Europe her independence and continued existence as a vital force for civilization in world affairs.

European Movement and the Council of Europe,
48–50. London, 1949

10 The North Atlantic Treaty, 4 April 1949

The Parties to this Treaty reaffirm their faith in the purposes and principles of the Charter of the United Nations and their desire to live in peace with all peoples and all governments.

They are determined to safeguard the freedom, common heritage and civilization of their peoples, founded on the principles of democracy, individual liberty and the rule of law.

They seek to promote stability and well-being in the North Atlantic area.

They are resolved to unite their efforts for collective defence and for the preservation of peace and security.

They therefore agree to this North Atlantic Treaty:

Article 1

The Parties undertake, as set forth in the Charter of the United Nations, to settle any international dispute in which they may be involved by peaceful means in such a manner that international peace and security and justice are not endangered, and to refrain in their international relations from the threat or use of force in any manner inconsistent with the purposes of the United Nations.

Article 2

The Parties will contribute towards the further development of peaceful and friendly international relations by strengthening their free institutions, by bringing about a better understanding of the principles upon which these institutions are founded, and by promoting conditions of stability and well-being. They will seek to eliminate conflict in their international economic policies and will encourage economic collaboration between any or all of them.

Article 3

In order more effectively to achieve the objectives of this Treaty, the Parties, separately and jointly, by means of continuous and effective self-help and mutual aid, will maintain and develop their individual and collective capacity to resist armed attack.

Article 4

The Parties will consult together whenever, in the opinion of any one of them, the territorial integrity, political independence or security of any of the Parties is threatened.

Article 5

The Parties agree that an armed attack against one or more of them in Europe or North America shall be considered an attack against them all and consequently they agree that, if such an armed attack occurs, each of them, in exercise of the right of individual or collective self-defence recognized by Article 51 of the Charter of the United Nations, will assist the Party or Parties so attacked by taking forthwith, individually and in concert with the other Parties, such action as it deems necessary, including the use of armed force, to restore and maintain the security of the North Atlantic area. Any such armed attack and all measures taken as a result thereof shall immediately be reported to the Security Council. Such measures shall be terminated when the Security Council has taken the measures necessary to restore and maintain international peace and security.

Article 6

For the purpose of Article 5 an armed attack on one or more of the Parties is deemed to include an armed attack on the territory of any of the Parties in Europe or North America . . . , on the occupation forces of any Party in Europe, on the islands under the jurisdiction of any Party in the North Atlantic area north of the Tropic of Cancer or on the vessels or aircraft in this area of any of the Parties.

Article 7

This Treaty does not affect, and shall not be interpreted as affecting, in any way the rights and obligations under the Charter of the Parties which are members of the United Nations, or the primary responsibility of the Security Council for the maintenance of international peace and security.

Article 8

Each Party declares that none of the international engagements now in force between it and any other of the Parties or any third State is in conflict with the provisions of this Treaty, and undertakes not to enter into any international engagement in conflict with this Treaty.

Article 9

The Parties hereby establish a Council, on which each of them shall be represented, to consider matters concerning the implementation of this Treaty. The Council shall be so organized as to be able to meet promptly at any time. The Council shall set up such subsidiary bodies as may be necessary; in particular it shall establish immediately a defence committee which shall recommend measures for the implementation of Articles 4 and 5.

Article 10

The Parties may, by unanimous agreement, invite any other European State in a position to further the principles of this Treaty and to contribute to the security of the North Atlantic area to accede to this Treaty. Any State so invited may become a Party to the Treaty by depositing its instrument of accession with the Government of the United States of America. The Government of the United States of America will inform each of the Parties of the deposit of each instrument of accession.

Article 11

This Treaty shall be ratified and its provisions carried out by the Parties in accordance with their respective constitutional processes. The instruments of ratification shall be deposited as soon as possible with the Government of the United States of America, which will notify all the other signatories of each deposit. The Treaty shall enter into force between the States which have ratified it as soon as the ratifications of the majority of the signatories, including the ratifications of Belgium, Canada, France, Luxembourg, the Netherlands, the United Kingdom and the United States, have been deposited and shall come into effect with respect to other States on the date of the deposit of their ratifications.

Article 12

After the Treaty has been in force for ten years, or at any time thereafter, the Parties shall, if any of them so requests, consult together for the purpose of reviewing the Treaty, having regard for the factors then affecting peace and security in the North Atlantic area, including the development of universal as well as regional arrangements under the Charter of the United Nations for the maintenance of international peace and security.

Article 13

After the Treaty has been in force for twenty years, any Party may cease to be a Party one year after its notice of denunciation has been given to the Government of the United States of America, which will inform the Governments of the other Parties of the deposit of each notice of denunciation.

Article 14

This Treaty, of which the English and French texts are equally authentic, shall be deposited in the archives of the Government of the United States of America. Duly certified copies will be transmitted by that Government to the governments of the other signatories.

NATO, Facts and figures, 270–3: Brussels, 1971

11   Statute of the Council of Europe with 1951 Amendments, 5 May 1949

The Governments of the Kingdom of Belgium, the Kingdom of Denmark, the French Republic, the Irish Republic, the Italian Republic, the Grand Duchy of Luxembourg, the Kingdom of the Netherlands, the Kingdom of Norway, the Kingdom of Sweden and the United Kingdom of Great Britain and Northern Ireland.

Convinced that the pursuit of peace based upon justice and international cooperation is vital for the preservation of human society and civilization;

Reaffirming their devotion to the spiritual and moral values which are the common heritage of their peoples and the true source of individual freedom, political liberty and the rule of law, principles which form the basis of all genuine democracy:

Believing that, for the maintenance and further realization of these ideals and in the interests of economic and social progress, there is need of a closer unity between all like-minded countries of Europe.

Considering that, to respond to this need and to the expressed aspirations of their peoples in this regard, it is necessary forthwith to create an organization which will bring European States into closer association;

Have in consequence decided to set up a Council of Europe consisting of a Committee of representatives of Governments and of a Consultative Assembly, and have for this purpose adopted the following Statute:

Article 1

(a) The aim of the Council of Europe is to achieve a greater unity between its Members for the purpose of safeguarding and realizing the ideals and principles which are their common heritage and facilitating their economic and social progress.

(b) This aim shall be pursued through the organs of the Council by discussion of questions of common concern and by agreements and common action in economic, social, cultural, scientific, legal and administrative matters and in the maintenance and further realization of human rights and fundamental freedoms.

(c) Participation in the Council of Europe shall not affect the collaboration of its Members in the work of the United Nations and of other international organizations or unions to which they are parties.

(d) Matters relating to National Defence do not fall within the scope of the Council of Europe. . . .

Article 3

Every Member of the Council of Europe must accept the principles of the rule of law and of the enjoyment by all persons within its jurisdiction of human rights and fundamental freedoms, and collaborate sincerely and effectively in the realization of the aim of the Council. . . .

Article 8

Any Member of the Council of Europe which has seriously violated Article 3 may be suspended from its rights of representation and requested by the Committee of Ministers to withdraw. . . . If such

Member does not comply with this request, the Committee may decide that it has ceased to be a Member of the Council as from such date as the Committee may determine. . . .

Article 10

The organs of the Council of Europe are:
  (i) the Committee of Ministers;
  (ii) the Consultative Assembly.

Both these organs shall be served by the Secretariat of the Council of Europe.

Article 11

The seat of the Council of Europe is at Strasbourg.

Article 12

The official languages of the Council of Europe are English and French. The rules of procedure of the Committee of Ministers and of the Consultative Assembly shall determine in what circumstances and under what conditions other languages may be used.

Article 13

The Committee of Ministers is the organ which acts on behalf of the Council of Europe in accordance with Articles 15 and 16.

Article 14

Each Member shall be entitled to one representative on the Committee of Ministers, and each representative shall be entitled to one vote. Representatives on the Committee shall be the Ministers for Foreign Affairs. When a Minister for Foreign Affairs is unable to be present or in other circumstances where it may be desirable, an alternate may be nominated to act for him, who shall, whenever possible, be a member of his Government.

Article 15

(a) On the recommendation of the Consultative Assembly or on its own initiative, the Committee of Ministers shall consider the action required to further the aim of the Council of Europe, including the conclusion of conventions or agreements and the adoption by Governments of a common policy with regard to particular matters. Its conclusions shall be communicated to Members by the Secretary General. . . .

Article 19

At each session of the Consultative Assembly the Committee of Ministers shall furnish the Assembly with statements of its activities, accompanied by appropriate documentation. . . .

Article 22

The Consultative Assembly is the deliberative organ of the Council of Europe. It shall debate matters within its competence under this Statute and present its conclusions, in the form of recommendations, to the Committee of Ministers.

Article 23

(a) The Consultative Assembly shall discuss, and may make recommendations upon, any matter within the aim and scope of the Council of Europe . . . which (i) is referred to it by the Committee of Ministers with a request for its opinion, or (ii) has been approved by the Committee for inclusion in the Agenda of the Assembly on the proposal of the latter.

(b) In taking decisions under (a), the Committee shall have regard to the work of other European inter-governmental organizations to which some or all of the Members of the Council are parties. . . .

(c) The President of the Assembly shall decide, in case of doubt, whether any question raised in the course of the Session is within the Agenda of the Assembly approved under (a) above. . . .

Article 25

(a) The Consultative Assembly shall consist of representatives of each Member appointed in such a manner as the Government of that Member shall decide. Each representative must be a national of the Member whom he represents, but shall not at the same time be a member of the Committee of Ministers.

(b) No representative shall be deprived of his position as such during a session of the Assembly without the agreement of the Assembly.

(c) Each representative may have a substitute who may, in the absence of the representative, sit, speak and vote in his place. The provisions of paragraph (a) above apply to the appointment of substitutes. . . .

Article 32

The Consultative Assembly shall meet in ordinary session once a year, the date and duration of which shall be determined by the Assembly so as to avoid as far as possible overlapping with parliamentary sessions of Members and with sessions of the General Assembly of the United Nations. In no circumstances shall the duration of an ordinary session exceed one month unless both the Assembly and the Committee of Ministers concur. . . .

Article 36

(a) The Secretariat shall consist of a Secretary General, a Deputy Secretary General and such other staff as may be required. . . .

Cmd. 7778. London, HMSO

12 Speech of Paul Hoffman to the OEEC Council in Paris, 31 October 1949

It has been fifteen months since I had the privilege of meeting with this council. In that period, Western Europe has made truly amazing progress in restoring its industrial and agricultural production. That progress is the result of work, hard work, on the part of millions of Europeans. That is the human story behind the cold statistics of production increase.

We applaud the success of your efforts. We in the Economic Cooperation Administration, and you in the Organization for European Economic Cooperation, have come to know each other well. Through working with you towards our common objectives we have come to hold the OEEC in high esteem, and our feeling toward its members is one of deep friendliness. I am delighted to be here, and I am pleased to note the presence of the representatives of the German Republic as full partners in your organization. It is as an admiring friend of the OEEC that I speak to you today.

Since 1947, we have confounded both the Communists and the other cynics by proving, first, that together we could successfully start economic recovery in Western Europe; and, second, that we could join in laying the foundations for security against attack upon our Atlantic community. We have seen anxiety give way to hope. Today I am asking you to turn hope into confidence.

The European Recovery Programme is now approaching the halfway mark. The time has come to consider carefully what more must be done to hold the ground already gained and to assure the further progress that is vitally needed. We must now devote our fullest energies to the major tasks.

These tasks are: First, to balance Europe's dollar accounts so that Europe can buy the raw materials and other items which mean employment and better living.

The second—and to say this is why I'm here—is to move ahead on a far-reaching programme to build in Western Europe a more dynamic, expanding economy which will promise steady improvement in the conditions of life for all its people. This, I believe, means nothing less than an integration of the Western European economy. . . .

Urgent as I regard the first major task—that of balancing Europe's trade with the dollar area—its performance will not be meaningful unless we have come to grips with our second task—the building of an expanding economy in Western Europe through economic integration.

The substance of such integration would be the formation of a single large market within which quantitative restrictions on the movement of goods, monetary barriers to the flow of payments and, eventually, all tariffs are permanently swept away. The fact that we have in the United States a single market of 150,000,000 consumers has been indispensable to the strength and efficiency of our economy. The creation of a permanent, freely trading area, comprising 270,000,000 consumers in Western Europe would have a multitude of helpful consequences. It would accelerate the development of large-scale, low-cost production industries. It would make the effective use of all resources easier, the stifling of healthy competition more difficult.

Obviously, such a step would not change the physical structure of European industry, or vastly increase productivity overnight, but the massive change in the economic environment would, I am convinced, set in motion a rapid growth in productivity. This would make it possible for Europe to improve its competitive position in the world and thus more nearly satisfy the expectations and needs of its people.

This is a vital objective. It was to this that Secretary Marshall pointed in the speech which sparked Europe to new hope and new endeavour. It was on this promise that the Congress of the United States enacted the ECA act. This goal is embedded in the convention of the OEEC.

I know that the difficulties which stand in the way of its achievement will spring all too readily to mind, but before integration is dismissed as a merely romantic possibility, too remote to have any bearing on practical, immediate decisions, I invite you to weigh the alternative. . . .

I do not believe that any path toward integration should be left unexplored. It seems to me absolutely essential that arrangements arrived at within groups of two, three, or more countries should be in harmony with wider possibilities of European unity and should, under no circumstances, involve the raising of new or higher barriers to trade within Europe than already exist.

I feel, therefore, that, while pressing forward to the broader objective of economic integration of all the participating countries, we should not slacken our efforts toward establishment of close economic arrangements within one or more small groups of countries— always with the intention that these should contribute toward, and not be turned against, the integration of the whole of Western Europe and its overseas territories.

I have made a number of references of the urgency of starting immediately on this programme of integration. My conviction on this point is based, in the first place, on the acute realization of the very short time still remaining during which American aid will be available to cushion the inevitable short-run dislocations which a programme of integration will involve. There is another very important reason for speed. The people and the Congress of the United States, and, I am sure, a great majority of the people of Europe, have instinctively felt that economic integration is essential if there is to be an end to Europe's recurring economic crises. A European programme to this end—one which should show real promise of taking this great forward step successfully—would, I strongly believe, give new impetus to American support for carrying through into 1952 our joint effort towards lasting European recovery.

For all these reasons—but particularly because of the urgency of the need—I do make this considered request: That you have ready early in 1950 a record of accomplishment and a programme, which together will take Europe well along the road towards economic integration.

By accomplishment I mean really effective action to remove the quantitative restrictions on trade on which you have recently made a start. I also mean the elimination in Europe of the unsound practice of double pricing—that is, maintaining export prices for fuel and basic materials at higher levels than domestic prices. This practice results in higher production costs throughout Europe. It cannot be squared with your pledges of mutual aid.

By a programme, I mean a realistic plan to meet the fundamental requirements I have described. Perhaps you will accomplish this through adaptation of existing institutions. Perhaps you will find that new central institutions are needed.

We are together playing for high stakes in this programme. The immediate goal is a solidly based prosperity for an economically unified Western Europe—a goal which President Truman reaffirmed to me just before I left Washington. Beyond that lies what has been the hope of all men of good-will during your lifetime and mine, an enduring peace founded on justice and freedom. That high hope can be realized if we, the people of the free world, continue to work together and stick together.

Text provided by the OECD and published with permission of the U.S. Department of State

III

The Six, 1950–1957

The historic French proposal for the pooling of the coal and steel industries of France and Germany, which was embodied in Robert Schuman's statement of 9 May 1950, has often been printed. Less well known is the memorandum (13) in which Jean Monnet set out the reasoning which lay behind the Schuman declaration. The ECSC which resulted had the most diverse origins. It even had a pre-war precursor in the International Steel Cartel, set up in 1926 by a group of private steel works, and re-established in 1933. In 1949 the Economic Commission for Europe of the United Nations published a report advocating an international steel authority; the creation of some kind of steel pool was discussed in the Council of Europe's Consultative Assembly at Strasbourg; and the Westminster Economic Conference had already recommended such a move. What eventually emerged in the Treaty of Paris of 18 April 1951 (16) was an agreement by six countries to set up a High Authority with supranational powers to administer their combined coal and steel industries: perhaps Europe's first authentically federal institution.

In the years that followed, under the presidency of Jean Monnet, this High Authority supervised the creation of common markets in coal and steel and the optimism it engendered led to proposals for other 'pools': a transport pool, an agricultural pool, and so on. The idea of 'integration by sector' gained currency and hard on the heels of the ECSC came the EDC, a plan for a European army which was first proposed by the French economist André Philip in the Consultative Assembly at Strasbourg in August 1950, and further elaborated in a statement by the French Prime Minister, René Pleven, acting on Monnet's suggestion, in the National Assembly, on 24 October 1950(14). The British response to this project of incorporating German contingents into a common European army, which the French had accepted because of American insistence on German rearmament, was unenthusiastic, as the Foreign Secretary, Ernest

Bevin, made abundantly clear in a House of Commons speech later that autumn (15). In the event it was the French who, on 30 August 1954, finally refused to ratify the treaty embodying the proposed EDC. After the failure of this project and as an alternative to it, the Western European Union was created by bringing West Germany and Italy into the Brussels Treaty Organization (6).

Article 38 of the EDC Treaty had provided for the creation of a European political community, and a draft treaty for this was published on 10 March 1953; but it, too, was never implemented. The double setback of 1954 was made good only slowly, and it was due to a further initiative by Jean Monnet, taken up by the Benelux powers, which proposed further developments to the other ECSC Member States in a Memorandum of 18 May 1955, that negotiations were started which finally led to the signature of the Treaty of Rome on 25 March 1957 (17) and the setting up of the European Economic Community by the same six countries who had joined to create the ECSC. This Community came into existence on 1 January 1958, at the same time as the European Atomic Energy Community (Euratom).

In this group of documents, the forward thrust of the Benelux powers, the braking action of Britain and important French initiatives are all well illustrated. It is notable that the most supranational of the four Communities mentioned here (ECSC, EDC, EPC, EEC) was the first to be established, the ECSC, while the two which were abandoned were perhaps the least supranational in character, *pace* Article 1 of the EPC treaty which blandly declared the EPC to be supranational although in fact what supranational character it had was to be provided by one of its constituent parts, namely the ECSC.

13 Memorandum sent by Jean Monnet to Robert Schuman and Georges Bidault, 4 May 1950

Wherever we look in the present world situation we see nothing but deadlock—whether it be the increasing acceptance of a war that is thought to be inevitable, the problem of Germany, the continuation of French recovery, the organization of Europe, the very place of France in Europe and in the world.

From such a situation there is only one way of escape: concrete, resolute action on a limited but decisive point, bringing about on this point a fundamental change, and gradually modifying the very terms of all the problems.

It is in this spirit that the attached proposal has been drawn up. The reflections below summarize the observations that led to it.

I

Men's minds are becoming focused on an object at once simple and dangerous: the cold war.

All proposals and all actions are interpreted by public opinion as a contribution to the cold war.

The cold war, whose essential objective is to make the opponent give way, is the first phase of real war.

This prospect creates among leaders a rigidity of mind that is characteristic of the pursuit of a single object. The search for solutions to problems ceases. This rigidity of mind and of objective, on both sides, leads inevitably to a clash, which is in the ineluctable logic of this way of looking at things. From this clash will come war.

In effect, we are already at war.

The course of events must be changed. To do this, men's minds must be changed. Words are not enough. Only immediate action on an essential point can change the present static situation. This action must be radical, real, immediate, and dramatic; it must change things and make a reality of the hopes which people are on the point of abandoning. And thereby give the peoples of the 'free' countries faith in the more distant goals that will be put to them, and the active determination to pursue them.

II

The German situation is rapidly becoming a cancer that will be dangerous to peace in the near future, and to France immediately, if its development is not directed towards hope for the Germans and collaboration with the free peoples.

This situation cannot be dealt with by the unification of Germany, for that would require an agreement between the USA and the USSR, which for the moment is impossible to conceive.

It cannot be dealt with by integrating Western Germany with the West,

—because the West Germans would thereby put themselves, *vis-à-vis* the East, in the position of having accepted separation, whereas unity must necessarily be their constant objective;
—because integration raises the question of arming Germany, and will lead to war by provoking the Russians;
—because of insoluble political problems.

And yet the Americans will insist on the integration of the West,
—because they want something to be done and have no other
idea on hand;
—because they doubt French solidity and dynamism. Some think
it necessary to start establishing a replacement for France.

We must not try to solve the German problem, which cannot be
solved in the present situation. We must change the context by
transforming it.

We must undertake a dynamic action which transforms the German
situation and gives direction to the minds of the Germans—not seek a
static solution based on things as they are.

III

The continuation of France's recovery will be halted if the question
of German industrial production and its competitive capacity is not
rapidly solved.

The basis of the superiority which French industrialists traditionally
recognize in Germany is her ability to produce steel at a price that
France cannot match. From this they conclude that the whole of
French production is thereby handicapped.

Already Germany is asking to increase her production from 11 to 14
million tons. We shall refuse, but the Americans will insist. Finally, we
shall state our reservations but we shall give in. At the same time,
French production is levelling off or even falling.

Merely to state these facts makes it unnecessary to describe in great
detail what the consequences will be: Germany expanding, German
dumping on export markets; a call for the protection of French
industries; the halting or camouflage of trade liberalization; the re-
establishment of pre-war cartels; perhaps an orientation of German
expansion towards the East, a prelude to political agreements; France
fallen back into the rut of limited, protected production. . . .

The USA do not want things to take this course. They will accept an
alternative solution if it is dynamic and constructive, especially if it is
proposed by France.

With the solution proposed there is no more question of
domination by German industry, which would create fear in Europe, a
source of constant troubles, and would finally prevent Europe being
unified and lead once more to the ruin of Germany herself. This
solution, on the contrary, creates for industry—German, French, and
European—the conditions for joint expansion, in competition but
without domination.

From the French point of view, such a solution gives French industry the same start as German industry; it eliminates the dumping on export markets which would otherwise be practised by the German steel industry; and it enables the French steel industry to participate in European expansion, without fear of dumping and without the temptation to form a cartel. Fear on the part of industrialists, which would lead to Malthusianism, to the halting of 'liberalization', and finally back to the well-worn ruts of the past, will be eliminated. The biggest obstacle to the continuation of French industrial progress will have been removed.

IV

Until now, we have been engaged in an effort to organize the West economically, militarily, and politically: OEEC, the Brussels Pact, Strasbourg.

Two years' experience, the discussions in OEEC on payments agreements, the liberalization of trade, etc., the armament programme submitted to the last Brussels meeting, the discussions in Strasbourg, the efforts—still without concrete results—to achieve a Franco-Italian customs union, all show that we are making no real progress towards the goal we have set ourselves, which is the organization of Europe, its economic development, and its collective security.

Britain, however anxious she may be to collaborate with Europe, will agree to nothing that might result in a loosening of her ties with the Dominions or a commitment to Europe going beyond those undertaken by America herself.

Germany, an essential element in Europe, cannot be drawn into the European organization in the present state of things, for the reasons given above.

It is certain that to continue the action undertaken along the lines we have adopted will lead to an impasse, and moreover may let slip the moment when this organization of Europe would have been possible.

As it is, the peoples of Europe hear nothing but words. Soon, they will no longer believe in the idea which Government persist in offering them, and which gets no further than empty speeches and futile meetings.

American public opinion will not support common action and American participation if Europe does not show itself dynamic.

For future peace, the creation of a dynamic Europe is indispensable. An association of the 'free' peoples, in which the USA will participate, does not exclude the building of Europe; on the contrary, because this association will be based on liberty, and therefore on diversity, Europe will, if it adapts to new conditions in the world, develop its creative abilities and thus, gradually, emerge as a stabilizing force.

We must therefore abandon the forms of the past and enter the path of transformation, both by creating common basic economic conditions and by setting up new authorities accepted by the sovereign nations.

Europe has never existed. It is not the addition of sovereign nations met together in councils that makes an entity of them. We must genuinely create Europe; it must become manifest to itself and to American public opinion; and it must have confidence in its own future.

This creation, at the moment when association with an America of such power is in question, is indispensable in order to make clear that the countries of Europe are not taking the easy way out, that they are not giving way to fear, that they believe in themselves, and that they are setting up without delay the first machinery for building a Europe within the new community of free and peaceful peoples, to which it will bring stability and the continuation of its creative thinking.

V

At the present moment, Europe can be brought to birth only by France. Only France can speak and act.

But if France does not speak and act now, what will happen?

A group will form around the United States, but in order to wage the cold war with greater force. The obvious reason is that the countries of Europe are afraid and are seeking help. Britain will draw closer and closer to the United States; Germany will develop rapidly, and we shall not be able to prevent her being armed. France will be trapped again in her former Malthusiansim, and this will lead inevitably to her being effaced.

VI

Since the Liberation, the French, far from being cast down by suffering, have shown vitality and faith in the future: increased production, modernization, the transformation of agriculture, the development of the French Union, etc.

During these years the French have forgotten Germany and German competition. They believed in peace. Suddenly they have rediscovered Germany and war.

The growth of German production, and the organization of the cold

war, would revive past fears and set off Malthusian reflexes. The
French would relapse into their old timidity, at the very moment when
boldness would enable them to eliminate these two dangers and cause
the French spirit to make the progress for which it is ready.

At this juncture, France is singled out by destiny. If she takes the
initiative that will eliminate fear, revive faith in the future, and make
possible the creation of a force for peace, she will have liberated
Europe. And in a liberated Europe, the spirit of men born on the soil
of France, living in freedom and in steadily improving material and
social conditions, will continue to make the contribution that is
essentially theirs.

> Text translated from the original and
> supplied by Dr Richard Mayne

14   The Pleven Plan (EDC) announced in the French National Assembly, 24 October 1950

Ladies and Gentlemen, the ideal of collective security has just achieved
a victory in Korea which marks an historic advance in the efforts of the
free nations to create in the world conditions of security such as to
discourage any aggressive designs.

The nations which concluded the Atlantic Treaty wished to forge the
instrument for that security for the region covered by the Treaty. They
have in the last few months achieved unprecedented progress in defining
their views on a common defence programme and embarking on the
implementation of those views. . . .

The associated nations have recognized the need to defend the
Atlantic community against any possible aggression, on a line situated
as far to the East as possible. They have decided to increase the forces
stationed in Europe for this purpose. They have agreed that all those
forces, irrespective of their nationality, should be placed under the
command of a single commander-in-chief. . . .

Germany, which is not a party to the Atlantic Treaty, is nevertheless
also destined to enjoy the benefits of the security system resulting
therefrom. It is consequently right that it should make its contribution
towards setting up a system of defence for Western Europe.
Consequently, before opening discussions on this important problem
in the Assembly, the [French] Government have decided to take the
initiative of making the following declaration. . . .

It proposes the creation, for our common defence, of a European
Army tied to political institutions of a united Europe.

This suggestion is directly inspired by the recommendations adopted on 11 August 1950 by the Assembly of the Council of Europe, demanding the immediate creation of a unified European Army destined to cooperate with the American and Canadian forces in the defence of peace.

The setting up of a European Army cannot result from a mere grouping together of national military units, which would in reality only mask a coalition of the old sort. For tasks which are inevitably common ones, only common institutions will do. The army of a united Europe, composed of men coming from different European countries, must, so far as is possible, achieve a complete fusion of the human and material elements which make it up under a single European political and military authority.

A Minister of Defence would be appointed by the participating governments and would be responsible, under conditions to be determined, to those appointing him and to a European Assembly. That assembly might be the Assembly in Strasbourg, or an offshoot thereof, or an assembly composed of specially elected delegates. His powers with respect to the European Army would be those of a national Minister of Defence with respect to the national forces of his own country. He would, in particular, be responsible for implementing such general directives as he might receive from a Council composed of Ministers of the participating countries. He would serve as the normal channel between the European community and outside countries or international organs for everything relating to the carrying out of his task.

The contingents furnished by the participating States would be incorporated in the European Army at the level of the smallest possible unit.

The money for the European Army would be provided by a common budget. The European Minister of Defence would be responsible for the implementation of existing international obligations and for the negotiation and implementation of new international engagements on the basis of directives received from the council of ministers. The European armament and equipment programme would be decided and carried out under his authority.

The participating States which currently have national forces at their disposal would retain their own authority so far as concerned that part of their existing forces which was not integrated by them into the European Army.

Conversely, the European Minister of Defence might, with the authorization of the Council of Ministers, place at the disposal of a participating government a part of its national forces comprised in the European force, for the purpose of meeting requirements other than those of common defence.

The European force placed at the disposal of the unified Atlantic Command would operate in accordance with the obligations assumed in the Atlantic Treaty, both so far as concerns general strategy and so far as concerns organization and equipment.

The European Minister of Defence would be responsible for obtaining from member countries of the European community the contingents, the equipment, the armaments, and the supplies due from each State to the common army.

During the establishment of this European Army a transitional phase will be necessary. During this period, a part of the existing national armies, although placed under the unified Atlantic Command, will probably not be capable of immediate incorporation into the European Army. The latter would have to develop progressively, each country furnishing its contribution of men, in proportions decided by the Council of Ministers and taking into account the general plan of defence drawn up by the Atlantic Council.

Finally, the creation of a European Army cannot, either in the initial phase or in its ultimate realization, in any way constitute a cause for delay in the implementation of programmes envisaged or under way within the Atlantic organization for the establishment of national forces under a unified command. On the contrary, the projected creation of the European Army should facilitate the implementation of the Atlantic programmes.

It is on the basis I have just sketched out that the French Government proposes to invite Great Britain and the free countries of continental Europe, should they agree to participate with it in the creation of a European Army, to work together on ways of realizing the principles just stated. Those studies would begin in Paris as soon as the coal and steel treaty is signed. . . .

> *Landmarks in European Unity*, ed. S. Patijn, 73–85 (translation by the Europa Instituut, Leiden)

15   Speech of the Foreign Secretary of the United Kingdom in a foreign affairs debate in the House of Commons, 29 November 1950

If, unhappily, aggression were to take place in Europe, we are satisfied that its defence would have to take place as far East as possible, and that means that Western Germany must be involved; and if Western Germany is to be defended, it seems to us only fair and reasonable that the people of Western Germany should help in their own defence.

Many people are quite understandably worried at the prospect of rearming Germany so shortly after the end of the war. They fear that the spirit of Nazism will rise again and, with it, a German Army and General Staff on the old model. That is a point of great anxiety to all the Governments and to everyone who has had to study this problem. But it is something which the rest of the Atlantic Powers could not tolerate. The present leaders of Germany are as strongly opposed as the Atlantic Powers to a re-creation of the German General Staff and of a German Army on the old model. Nevertheless, we cannot risk such a danger. We therefore agreed with the Americans that any German contribution to the defence of Western Europe must be in the form of units in the integrated Atlantic Force. The French Government were unable to accept this proposal and the New York meeting had to break up without reaching any final agreement.

The French Government have now produced a proposal for a European Army with a European Minister of Defence, subject to a European Council of Ministers and a European Assembly. This European Army would contain German units as well as units from the other European countries. His Majesty's Government do not favour this proposal. To begin with, we fear that it will only delay the building up of Europe's defences. Our first and most urgent need is to set up the integrated Force under the Supreme Commander. The next step is to provide for a German contribution to that force. These are immediate matters of great urgency. We take the view that the proposal for a European Army is also too limited in scope. We cherish our special ties with our old European friends but, in our view, Europe is not enough; it is not big enough, it is not strong enough and it is not able to stand by itself.

I understand the urge towards European unity and sympathize with it and, indeed, I did much to help bring the Council of Europe into being. But I also understand the new paradox that European unity is no longer possible within Europe alone but only within the broader Atlantic community. It is this great conception of an Atlantic community that we want to build up. This union of twelve free, equal and independent nations, organized for the defence of peace and for the growth of prosperity, comprising most of the free nations of Europe and working in harmony with the aims and purposes of the United Nations, is a great new force in the world. It includes two

Commonwealth countries, Canada and ourselves, who will always work in the closest association with the other members of the Commonwealth.

We have set our hopes on this conception. We want it to develop far beyond its immediate purpose of defence into a lasting association of like-minded nations. That is why, I am sorry to say, we cannot accept the French proposal. That is why His Majesty's Government, looking at the problem of the future security of the West, are in favour of the Atlantic conception. Nevertheless, if it is the wish of the French Government and of other Governments in Europe to proceed to examine the possibilities of forming a European Army as a part of the integrated force for the defence of Europe, His Majesty's Government would not stand in their way.

We are trying to reconcile the different approach caused by our geographical position, our international responsibilities, our Commonwealth connection and every other factor concerned, and we are not at loggerheads with the French. If the French, with their long tradition and their European view, take one line regarding Europe and if they will not try to force us into an awkward position, we certainly will put no pressure on them with regard to their desire for a European Army. But I repeat what I said, and I appeal to them to let us get on. We are anxious to avoid delay. The situation in the world is very dangerous. All peoples can combine on this problem of security and peace. It is in the interests of all of us in Western Europe that the solution should be found promptly, and security assured. . . .

Hansard. Parliamentary Debates, vol. 481, cols.
1172–4, London, 1950

16   Treaty establishing the ECSC, 18 April 1951

The President of the Federal Republic of Germany, His Royal Highness the Prince Royal of Belgium, the President of the French Republic, the President of the Italian Republic, Her Royal Highness the Grand Duchess of Luxembourg, Her Majesty the Queen of the Netherlands,

Considering that world peace can be safeguarded only by creative efforts commensurate with the dangers that threaten it,

Convinced that the contribution which an organized and vital Europe can make to civilization is indispensable to the maintenance of peaceful relations,

Recognizing that Europe can be built only through practical

achievements which will first of all create real solidarity, and through the establishment of common bases for economic development,

Anxious to help, by expanding their basic production, to raise the standard of living and further the works of peace,

Resolved to substitute for age-old rivalries the merging of their essential interests; to create, by establishing an economic community, the basis for a broader and deeper community among peoples long divided by bloody conflicts; and to lay the foundations for institutions which will give direction to a destiny henceforward shared,

Have decided to create a European Coal and Steel Community and to this end have designated as their plenipotentiaries:

The President of the Federal Republic of Germany:
  Dr Konrad Adenauer, Chancellor and
  Minister for Foreign Affairs;

His Royal Highness the Prince Royal of Belgium:
  Mr Paul Van Zeeland, Minister for Foreign Affairs,
  Mr Joseph Meurice, Minister for Foreign Trade;

The President of the French Republic:
  Mr Robert Schuman, Minister for Foreign Affairs;

The President of the Italian Republic:
  Mr Carlo Sforza, Minister for Foreign Affairs;

Her Royal Highness the Grand Duchess of Luxembourg:
  Mr Joseph Bech, Minister for Foreign Affairs;

Her Majesty the Queen of the Netherlands:
  Mr D. U. Stikker, Minister for Foreign Affairs,
  Mr J. R. M. Van Den Brink, Minister for Economic Affairs;
who, having exchanged their Full Powers, found in good and due form, have agreed as follows:

Article 1

By this Treaty, the High Contracting Parties establish among themselves a European Coal and Steel Community, founded upon a common market, common objectives and common institutions.

Article 2

The European Coal and Steel Community shall have as its task to contribute, in harmony with the general economy of the Member States and through the establishment of a common market as provided in Article 4, to economic expansion, growth of employment and a rising standard of living in the Member States.

The Community shall progressively bring about conditions which will of themselves ensure the most rational distribution of production at the highest possible level of productivity, while safeguarding continuity of employment and taking care not to provoke fundamental and persistent disturbances in the economies of Member States.

Article 3

The institutions of the Community shall, within the limits of their respective powers, in the common interest:

(a) ensure an orderly supply to the common market, taking into account the needs of third countries;

(b) ensure that all comparably placed consumers in the common market have equal access to the sources of production;

(c) ensure the establishment of the lowest prices under such conditions that these prices do not result in higher prices charged by the same undertakings in other transactions or in a higher general price level at another time, while allowing necessary amortization and normal return on invested capital;

(d) ensure the maintenance of conditions which will encourage undertakings to expand and improve their production potential and to promote a policy of using natural resources rationally and avoiding their unconsidered exhaustion;

(e) promote improved working conditions and an improved standard of living for the workers in each of the industries for which it is responsible, so as to make possible their harmonization while the improvement is being maintained;

(f) promote the growth of international trade and ensure that equitable limits are observed in export pricing;

(g) promote the orderly expansion and modernization of production, and the improvement of quality, with no protection against competing industries that is not justified by improper action on their part or in their favour.

Article 4

The following are recognized as incompatible with the common market for coal and steel and shall accordingly be abolished and prohibited within the Community, as provided in this Treaty:

(a) import and export duties, or charges having equivalent effect, and quantitative restrictions on the movement of products;

(b) measures or practices which discriminate between producers,

between purchasers or between consumers, especially in prices
and delivery terms or transport rates and conditions, and
measures or practices which interfere with the purchaser's free
choice of supplier;

(c) subsidies or aids granted by States, or special charges imposed
by States, in any form whatsoever;

(d) restrictive practices which tend towards the sharing or
exploiting of markets.

Article 5

The Community shall carry out its task in accordance with this
Treaty, with a limited measure of intervention.

To this end the Community shall:

—provide guidance and assistance for the parties concerned, by
obtaining information, organizing consultations and laying
down general objectives;

—place financial resources at the disposal of undertakings for their
investment and bear part of the cost of readaptation;

—ensure the establishment, maintenance and observance of normal
competitive conditions and exert direct influence upon
production or upon the market only when circumstances so
require;

—publish the reasons for its actions and take the necessary measures
to ensure the observance of the rules laid down in this Treaty.

The institutions of the Community shall carry out these activities
with a minimum of administrative machinery and in close cooperation
with the parties concerned.

Article 6

The Community shall have legal personality.

In international relations, the Community shall enjoy the legal
capacity it requires to perform its functions and attain its objectives.

In each of the Member States, the Community shall enjoy the most
extensive legal capacity accorded to legal persons constituted in that
State; it may, in particular, acquire or dispose of movable and
immovable property and may be a party to legal proceedings.

The Community shall be represented by its institutions, each within
the limits of its powers.

Article 7

The institutions of the Community shall be:
    a High Authority, assisted by a Consultative Committee;
    a Common Assembly (hereinafter called the 'Assembly');
    a Special Council of Ministers (hereinafter called the 'Council');
    a Court of Justice (hereinafter called the 'Court').

THE HIGH AUTHORITY

Article 8

It shall be the duty of the High Authority to ensure that the objectives set out in this Treaty are attained in accordance with the provisions thereof.

Article 9

The High Authority shall consist of nine members appointed for six years and chosen on the grounds of their general competence.

Retiring members may be reappointed. The number of members of the High Authority may be reduced by decision of the Council, acting unanimously.

Only nationals of Member States may be members of the High Authority.

The High Authority may not include more than two members having the nationality of the same State.

The members of the High Authority shall, in the general interest of the Community, be completely independent in the performance of their duties. In the performance of these duties, they shall neither seek nor take instructions from any Government or from any other body. They shall refrain from any action incompatible with the supranational character of their duties.

Each member State undertakes to respect this supranational character and not to seek to influence the members of the High Authority in the performance of their tasks.

The Members of the High Authority may not engage in any other occupation, whether gainful or not, nor may they acquire or hold, directly or indirectly, any interest in any business related to coal and steel during their term of office and for three years after ceasing to hold office. . . .

Article 11

The President and Vice-President of the High Authority shall be appointed from among its members for a term of two years in accordance with the same procedure as that laid down for the appointment of members of the High Authority by the Governments of the Member States. Their appointments may be renewed.

Save where the entire High Authority is replaced, such appointments shall be made after the High Authority has been consulted.

Article 12

Apart from normal replacement, the appointment of a member of the High Authority shall end on his death or retirement.

Members who no longer fulfil the conditions required for the performance of their duties or who are guilty of serious misconduct may be compulsorily retired by the Court, on application by the High Authority or the Council. . . .

Article 13

The High Authority shall act by a majority of its members.

The rules of procedure shall determine the quorum. This quorum, however, must be greater than one half of the membership of the High Authority.

Article 14

In order to carry out the tasks assigned to it the High Authority shall, in accordance with the provisions of this Treaty, take decisions, make recommendations or deliver opinions.

Decisions shall be binding in their entirety.

Recommendations shall be binding as to the aims to be pursued but shall leave the choice of the appropriate methods for achieving these aims to those to whom the recommendations are addressed.

Opinions shall have no binding force.

In cases where the High Authority is empowered to take a decision, it may confine itself to making a recommendation. . . .

Article 18

A Consultative Committee shall be attached to the High Authority. It shall consist of not less than thirty and not more than fifty-one members and shall comprise equal numbers of producers, of workers, and of consumers and dealers.

The members of the Consultative Committee shall be appointed by the Council.

In the case of the producers and workers, the Council shall designate representative organizations among which it shall allocate the seats to be filled. Each organization shall be required to draw up a list containing twice as many names as there are seats allotted to it. Appointments shall be made from this list.

The members of the Consultative Committee shall be appointed in their personal capacity for two years. They shall not be bound by any mandate or instructions from the organizations which nominated them. . . .

THE ASSEMBLY

Article 20

The Assembly, which shall consist of representatives of the peoples of the States brought together in the Community, shall exercise the supervisory powers which are conferred upon it by this Treaty.

Article 21

The Assembly shall consist of delegates who shall be designated by the respective Parliaments once a year from among their members, or who shall be elected by direct universal suffrage, in accordance with the procedure laid down by each High Contracting Party.

The number of these delegates shall be as follows:

Germany	18
Belgium	10
France	18
Italy	18
Luxembourg	4
Netherlands	10

The representatives of the population of the Saar are included in the number of delegates allotted to France.

Article 22

The Assembly shall hold an annual session. It shall meet, without requiring to be convened, on the second Tuesday in May. The session may not last beyond the end of the current financial year.

The Assembly may be convened in extraordinary session at the request of the Council in order to deliver an opinion on such questions as may be put to it by the Council.

It may also meet in extraordinary session at the request of a majority of its members or of the High Authority. . . .

Article 24

The Assembly shall discuss in open session the general report submitted to it by the High Authority.

If a motion of censure on the report is tabled before it, the Assembly shall not vote thereon until at least three days after the motion has been tabled and only by open vote.

If the motion of censure is carried by a two-thirds majority of the votes cast, representing a majority of the Members of the Assembly, the members of the High Authority shall resign as a body. . . .

THE COUNCIL

Article 26

The Council shall exercise its powers in the cases provided for and in the manner set out in this Treaty, in particular in order to harmonize the action of the High Authority and that of the Governments, which are responsible for the general economic policies of their countries.

To this end, the Council and the High Authority shall exchange information and consult each other.

The Council may request the High Authority to examine any proposals or measures which the Council may consider appropriate or necessary for the attainment of the common objectives.

Article 27

The Council shall consist of representatives of the Member States. Each State shall delegate to it one of the members of its Government.

The office of President shall be held for a term of three months by each member of the Council in turn, in the alphabetical order of the Member States.

Article 28

The Council shall meet when convened by its President at the request of a Member State or of the High Authority.

When the Council is consulted by the High Authority, it shall consider the matter without necessarily taking a vote. The minutes of its proceedings shall be forwarded to the High Authority.

Wherever this Treaty requires the assent of the Council, that assent shall be considered to have been given if the proposal submitted by the High Authority receives the approval:

— of an absolute majority of the representatives of the Member States, including the vote of the representative of one of the States which each produce at least one sixth of the total value of the coal and steel output of the Community; or

— in the event of an equal division of votes and if the High Authority maintains its proposal after a second discussion, of the representatives of the two Member States which each produce at least 20 per cent of the total value of the coal and steel output of the Community.

Wherever this Treaty requires a unanimous decision or unanimous assent, such decision or assent shall be duly given if all the members of the Council vote in favour.

Decisions of the Council, other than those which require a qualified majority or unanimity, shall be taken by a vote of the majority of its members; this majority shall be considered to be attained if it represents an absolute majority of the representatives of the Member States, including the vote of the representative of one of the States which each produce at least 20 per cent of the total value of the coal and steel output of the Community.

Where a vote is taken, any member of the Council may also act on behalf of not more than one other Member.

The Council shall deal with the Member States through its President.

The acts of the Council shall be published in such a manner as it may decide. . . .

THE COURT

Article 31

The Court shall ensure that in the interpretation and application of this Treaty, and of rules laid down for the implementation thereof, the law is observed.

Article 32

The Court shall consist of seven Judges appointed by common accord of the Governments of the Member States for a term of six years from persons whose independence and competence are beyond doubt.

Every three years there shall be a partial replacement, three and four members being replaced alternately. The three members whose terms of office are to expire at the end of the first three years shall be chosen by lot.

Retiring Judges shall be eligible for reappointment.

The number of Judges may be increased by the Council, acting unanimously on a proposal from the Court.

The Judges shall elect the President of the Court from among their number for a term of three years. . . .

ECONOMIC AND SOCIAL CONDITIONS

Article 46

The High Authority may at any time consult Governments, the various parties concerned (undertakings, workers, consumers and dealers) and their associations, and any experts.

Undertakings, workers, consumers and dealers, and their associations, shall be entitled to present any suggestions or comments to the High Authority on questions affecting them.

To provide guidance, in line with the tasks assigned to the Community, on the course of action to be followed by all concerned, and to determine its own course of action, in accordance with the provisions of this Treaty, the High Authority shall, in consultation as provided above:

(1) conduct a continuous study of market and price trends;

(2) periodically draw up programmes indicating foreseeable developments in production, consumption, exports and imports;

(3) periodically lay down general objectives for modernization, long-term planning of manufacture and expansion of productive capacity;

(4) take part, at the request of the Governments concerned, in studying the possibilities of re-employing, in existing industries or through the creation of new activities, workers made redundant by market developments or technical changes;

(5) obtain the information it requires to assess the possibilities for improving working conditions and living standards for workers in the industries within its province, and the threats to those standards.

The High Authority shall publish the general objectives and the programmes after submitting them to the Consultative Committee.

It may publish the studies and information mentioned above.

Article 47

The High Authority may obtain the information it requires to carry out its tasks. It may have any necessary checks made.

The High Authority must not disclose information of the kind covered by the obligation of professional secrecy, in particular information about undertakings, their business relations or their cost components. Subject to this reservation, it shall publish such data as could be useful to Governments or to any other parties concerned.

The High Authority may impose fines or periodic penalty payments on undertakings which evade their obligations under decisions taken in pursuance of this Article or which knowingly furnish false information. The maximum amount of such fines shall be 1 per cent of the annual turnover, and the maximum amount of such penalty payments shall be 5 per cent of the average daily turnover for each day's delay. . . .

Article 48

The right of undertakings to form associations shall not be affected by this Treaty. Membership of such associations must be voluntary. Associations may engage in any activity which is not contrary to the provisions of this Treaty or to the decisions or recommendations of the High Authority. . . .

Article 49

The High Authority is empowered to procure the funds it requires to carry out its tasks:

—by imposing levies on the production of coal and steel;
—by contracting loans.

It may receive gifts. . . .

Article 54

The High Authority may facilitate the carrying out of investment programmes by granting loans to undertakings or by guaranteeing other loans which they may contract.

With the unanimous assent of the Council, the High Authority may by the same means assist the financing of works and installations which contribute directly and primarily to increasing the production, reducing the production costs or facilitating the marketing of products within its jurisdiction.

Article 55

1. The High Authority shall promote technical and economic research relating to the production and increased use of coal and steel and to occupational safety in the coal and steel industries. To this end it shall organize all appropriate contacts among existing research bodies. . . .

Article 57

In the sphere of production, the High Authority shall give preference to the indirect means of action at its disposal, such as:

—cooperation with Governments to regularize or influence general consumption, particularly that of public services;
—intervention in regard to prices and commercial policy as provided for in this Treaty. . . .

Article 60

1. Pricing practices contrary to Articles 2, 3 and 4 shall be prohibited, in particular:
—unfair competitive practices, especially purely temporary or purely local price reductions tending towards the acquisition of a monopoly position within the common market;
—discriminatory practices involving, within the common market, the application by a seller of dissimilar conditions to comparable transactions, especially on grounds of the nationality of the buyer.

The High Authority may define the practices covered by this prohibition by decisions taken after consulting the Consultative Committee and the Council.

Article 61

On the basis of studies made jointly with undertakings and associations of undertakings . . . and after consulting the Consultative Committee and the Council as to the advisability of so doing and the price level to be so determined, the High Authority may, for one or more of the products within its jurisdiction:

(a) fix maximum prices within the common market, if it finds that such a decision is necessary to attain the objectives set out in Article 3, and particularly in paragraph (c) thereof;

(b) fix minimum prices within the common market, if it finds that a manifest crisis exists or is imminent and that such a decision is necessary to attain the objectives set out in Article 3;

(c) after consulting the associations to which the undertakings concerned belong, or the undertakings themselves, fix, by methods appropriate to the nature of the export markets, minimum or maximum export prices. . . .

Article 63

1. If the High Authority finds that discrimination is being systematically practised by purchasers, in particular under provisions governing contracts entered into by bodies dependent on a public authority, it shall make appropriate recommendations to the Governments concerned. . . .

Article 65

1. All agreements between undertakings, decisions by associations of undertakings and concerted practices tending directly or indirectly to prevent, restrict or distort normal competition within the common market shall be prohibited, and in particular those tending:

(a) to fix or determine prices;

(b) to restrict or control production, technical development or investments;

(c) to share markets, products, customers or sources of supply.

2. However, the High Authority shall authorize specialization agreements or joint-buying or joint-selling agreements in respect of particular products. . . .

Article 70

It is recognized that the establishment of the common market necessitates the application of such rates and conditions for the carriage of coal and steel as will afford comparable price conditions to comparably placed consumers.

Any discrimination in rates and conditions of carriage of every kind which is based on the country of origin or destination of products shall be prohibited in traffic between Member States. For the purpose of eliminating such discrimination it shall in particular be obligatory to apply to the carriage of coal and steel to or from another country of the Community the scales, rates and all other tariff rules of every kind which are applicable to the internal carriage of the same goods on the same route.

The scales, and rates and all other tariff rules of every kind applied to the carriage of coal and steel within each Member State and between Member States shall be published or brought to the knowledge of the High Authority. . . .

Article 83

The establishment of the Community shall in no way prejudice the system of ownership of the undertakings to which this Treaty applies. . . .

Article 97

This Treaty is concluded for a period of fifty years from its entry into force.

Article 98

Any European State may apply to accede to this Treaty. It shall address its application to the Council, which shall act unanimously after obtaining the opinion of the High Authority; the Council shall also determine the terms of accession, likewise acting unanimously. Accession shall take effect on the day when the instrument of accession is received by the Government acting as depositary of this Treaty.

Cmnd. 4863. London, HMSO

17   The Treaty of Rome, establishing the EEC, 25 March 1957

His Majesty the King of the Belgians, the President of the Federal Republic of Germany, the President of the French Republic, the President of the Italian Republic, Her Royal Highness the Grand Duchess of Luxembourg, Her Majesty the Queen of the Netherlands,

Determined to lay the foundations of an ever closer union among the peoples of Europe,

Resolved to ensure the economic and social progress of their countries by common action to eliminate the barriers which divide Europe,

Affirming as the essential objective of their efforts the constant improvement of the living and working conditions of their peoples,

Recognizing that the removal of existing obstacles calls for concerted action in order to guarantee steady expansion, balanced trade and fair competition,

Anxious to strengthen the unity of their economies and to ensure their harmonious development by reducing the differences existing between the various regions and the backwardness of the less favoured regions,

Desiring to contribute, by means of a common commercial policy, to the progressive abolition of restrictions on international trade,

Intending to confirm the solidarity which binds Europe and the overseas countries and desiring to ensure the development of their prosperity, in accordance with the principles of the Charter of the United Nations,

Resolved by thus pooling their resources to preserve and strengthen peace and liberty, and calling upon the other peoples of Europe who share their ideal to join in their efforts,

Have decided to create a European Economic Community and to this end have designated as their Plenipotentiaries:

His Majesty the King of the Belgians:

    Mr Paul-Henri Spaak, Minister for Foreign Affairs,

    Baron J. Ch. Snoy et d'Oppuers, Secretary-General of the Ministry of Economic Affairs, Head of the Belgian Delegation to the Intergovernmental Conference;

The President of the Federal Republic of Germany:

    Dr Konrad Adenauer, Federal Chancellor,

    Professor Dr Walter Hallstein, State Secretary of the Federal Foreign Office;

The President of the French Republic:

    Mr Christian Pineau, Minister for Foreign Affairs,

    Mr Maurice Faure, Under-Secretary of State for Foreign Affairs;

The President of the Italian Republic:

    Mr Antonio Segni, President of the Council of Ministers,

    Professor Gaetano Martino, Minister for Foreign Affairs;

Her Royal Highness the Grand Duchess of Luxembourg:

    Mr Joseph Bech, President of the Government, Minister for Foreign Affairs,

    Mr Lambert Schaus, Ambassador, Head of the Luxembourg Delegation to the Intergovernmental Conference;

Her Majesty the Queen of the Netherlands:

    Mr Joseph Luns, Minister for Foreign Affairs,

    Mr J. Linthorst Homan, Head of the Netherlands Delegation to the Intergovernmental Conference;

who, having exchanged their Full Powers, found in good and due form, have agreed as follows:

Article 1

By this Treaty, the High Contracting Parties establish among themselves a European Economic Community.

Article 2

The Community shall have as its task, by establishing a common market and progressively approximating the economic policies of Member States, to promote throughout the Community a harmonious development of economic activities, a continuous and balanced expansion, an increase in stability, an accelerated raising of the standard of living and closer relations between the States belonging to it.

Article 3

For the purposes set out in Article 2, the activities of the Community shall include, as provided in this Treaty and in accordance with the timetable set out therein:

(a) the elimination, as between Member States, of customs duties and of quantitative restrictions on the import and export of goods, and of all other measures having equivalent effect;

(b) the establishment of a common customs tariff and of a common commercial policy towards third countries;

(c) the abolition, as between Member States, of obstacles to freedom of movement for persons, services and capital;

(d) the adoption of a common policy in the sphere of agriculture;

(e) the adoption of a common policy in the sphere of transport;

(f) the institution of a system ensuring that competition in the common market is not distorted;

(g) the application of procedures by which the economic policies of Member States can be coordinated and disequilibria in their balances of payments remedied;

(h) the approximation of the laws of Member States to the extent required for the proper functioning of the common market;

(i) the creation of a European Social Fund in order to improve employment opportunities for workers and to contribute to the raising of their standard of living;

(j) the establishment of a European Investment Bank to facilitate the economic expansion of the Community by opening up fresh resources;

(k) the association of the overseas countries and territories in order to increase trade and to promote jointly economic and social development.

Article 4

1. The tasks entrusted to the Community shall be carried out by the following institutions:

—an Assembly,
—a Council,
—a Commission,
—a Court of Justice.

Each institution shall act within the limits of the powers conferred upon it by this Treaty.

2. The Council and the Commission shall be assisted by an Economic and Social Committee acting in an advisory capacity.

Article 5

Member States shall take all appropriate measures, whether general or particular, to ensure fulfilment of the obligations arising out of this Treaty or resulting from action taken by the institutions of the Community. They shall facilitate the achievement of the Community's tasks.

They shall abstain from any measure which could jeopardize the attainment of the objectives of this Treaty.

Article 6

1. Member States shall, in close cooperation with the institutions of the Community, coordinate their respective economic policies to the extent necessary to attain the objectives of this Treaty.

2. The institutions of the Community shall take care not to prejudice the internal and external financial stability of the Member States.

Article 7

Within the scope of application of this Treaty, and without prejudice to any special provisions contained therein, any discrimination on grounds of nationality shall be prohibited.

The Council may, on a proposal from the Commission and after consulting the Assembly, adopt, by a qualified majority, rules designed to prohibit such discrimination.

Article 8

1. The common market shall be progressively established during a transitional period of twelve years.

This transitional period shall be divided into three stages of four years each; the length of each stage may be altered in accordance with the provisions set out below.

2. To each stage there shall be assigned a set of actions to be initiated and carried through concurrently.

3. Transition from the first to the second stage shall be conditional upon a finding that the objectives specifically laid down in this Treaty for the first stage have in fact been attained in substance and that, subject to the exceptions and procedures provided for in this Treaty, the obligations have been fulfilled.

This finding shall be made at the end of the fourth year by the Council, acting unanimously on a report from the Commission. A Member State may not, however, prevent unanimity by relying upon the non-fulfilment of its own obligations. Failing unanimity, the first stage shall automatically be extended for one year.

At the end of the fifth year, the Council shall make its finding under the same conditions. Failing unanimity, the first stage shall automatically be extended for a further year.

At the end of the sixth year, the Council shall make its finding, acting by a qualified majority on a report from the Commission. . . .

FREE MOVEMENT OF GOODS

Article 9

1. The Community shall be based upon a customs union which shall cover all trade in goods and which shall involve the prohibition between Member States of customs duties on imports and exports and of all charges having equivalent effect, and the adoption of a common customs tariff in their relations with third countries. . . .

Article 12

Member States shall refrain from introducing between themselves any new customs duties on imports or exports or any charges having equivalent effect, and from increasing those which they already apply in their trade with each other.

Article 13

1. Customs duties on imports in force between Member States shall be progressively abolished by them during the transitional period in accordance with Articles 14 and 15.

2. Charges having an effect equivalent to customs duties on imports, in force between Member States, shall be progressively abolished by them during the transitional period. The Commission shall determine by means of directives the timetable for such abolition. It shall be guided by the rules contained in Article 14 (2) and (3) and by the directives issued by the Council pursuant to Article 14 (2).

Article 14

1. For each product, the basic duty to which the successive reductions shall be applied shall be the duty applied on 1 January 1957.

2. The timetable for the reductions shall be determined as follows:

(a) during the first stage, the first reduction shall be made one year after the date when this Treaty enters into force; the second reduction, eighteen months later; the third reduction, at the end of the fourth year after the date when this Treaty enters into force;

(b) during the second stage, a reduction shall be made eighteen months after that stage begins; a second reduction, eighteen months after the preceding one; a third reduction, one year later;

(c) any remaining reductions shall be made during the third stage; the Council shall, acting by a qualified majority on a proposal from the Commission, determine the timetable therefor by means of directives.

3. At the time of the first reduction, Member States shall introduce between themselves a duty on each product equal to the basic duty minus 10 per cent.

At the time of each subsequent reduction, each Member State shall reduce its customs duties as a whole in such manner as to lower by 10 per cent its total customs receipts as defined in paragraph 4 and to reduce the duty on each product by at least 5 per cent of the basic duty.

In the case, however, of products on which the duty is still in excess of 30 per cent, each reduction must be at least 10 per cent of the basic duty.

4. The total customs receipts of each Member State, as referred to in paragraph 3, shall be calculated by multiplying the value of its imports from other Member States during 1956 by the basic duties.

5. Any special problems raised in applying paragraphs 1 to 4 shall be settled by directives issued by the Council acting by a qualified majority on a proposal from the Commission.

6. Member States shall report to the Commission on the manner in which effect has been given to the preceding rules for the reduction of duties. They shall endeavour to ensure that the reduction made in the duties on each product shall amount:

—at the end of the first stage, to at least 25 per cent of the basic duty;
—at the end of the second stage, to at least 50 per cent of the basic duty.

If the Commission finds that there is a risk that the objectives laid down in Article 13, and the percentages laid down in this paragraph, cannot be attained, it shall make all appropriate recommendations to Member States.

7. The provisions of this Article may be amended by the Council, acting unanimously on a proposal from the Commission and after consulting the Assembly.

Article 15

1. Irrespective of the provisions of Article 14, any Member State may, in the course of the transitional period, suspend in whole or in part the collection of duties applied by it to products imported from other Member States. It shall inform the other Member States and the Commission thereof.

2. The Member States declare their readiness to reduce customs duties against the other Member States more rapidly than is provided for in Article 14 if their general economic situation and the situation of the economic sector concerned so permit.

To this end, the Commission shall make recommendations to the Member States concerned.

Article 16

Member States shall abolish between themselves customs duties on exports and charges having equivalent effect by the end of the first stage at the latest.

Article 17

1. The provisions of Articles 9 to 15 (1) shall also apply to customs duties of a fiscal nature. Such duties shall not, however, be taken into consideration for the purpose of calculating either total customs receipts or the reduction of customs duties as a whole as referred to in Article 14 (3) and (4).

Such duties shall, at each reduction, be lowered by not less than 10 per cent of the basic duty. Member States may reduce such duties more rapidly than is provided for in Article 14.

2. Member States shall, before the end of the first year after the entry into force of this Treaty, inform the Commission of their customs duties of a fiscal nature.

3. Member States shall retain the right to substitute for these duties an internal tax which complies with the provisions of Article 95.

4. If the Commission finds that substitution for any customs duty of a fiscal nature meets with serious difficulties in a Member State, it shall authorize that State to retain the duty on condition that it shall abolish it not later than six years after the entry into force of this Treaty. Such authorization must be applied for before the end of the first year after the entry into force of this Treaty.

Article 18

The Member States declare their readiness to contribute to the development of international trade and the lowering of barriers to trade by entering into agreements designed, on a basis of reciprocity and mutual advantage, to reduce customs duties below the general level of which they could avail themselves as a result of the establishment of a customs union between them.

Article 19

1. Subject to the conditions and within the limits provided for hereinafter, duties in the common customs tariff shall be at the level of the arithmetical average of the duties applied in the four customs territories comprised in the Community. . . .

Article 30

Quantitative restrictions on imports and all measures having equivalent effect shall, without prejudice to the following provisions, be prohibited between Member States.

Article 31

Member States shall refrain from introducing between themselves any new quantitative restrictions or measures having equivalent effect.

This obligation shall, however, relate only to the degree of liberalization attained in pursuance of the decisions of the Council of the OEEC of 14 January 1955. Member States shall supply the Commission, not later than six months after the entry into force of this Treaty, with lists of the products liberalized by them in pursuance of these decisions. These lists shall be consolidated between Member States.

Article 32

In their trade with one another Member States shall refrain from making more restrictive the quotas and measures having equivalent effect existing at the date of the entry into force of this Treaty.

These quotas shall be abolished by the end of the transitional period at the latest. During that period, they shall be progressively abolished in accordance with the following provisions.

Article 33

1. One year after the entry into force of this Treaty, each Member State shall convert any bilateral quotas open to any other Member States into global quotas open without discrimination to all other Member States.

On the same date, Member States shall increase the aggregate of the global quotas so established in such a manner as to bring about an increase of not less than 20 per cent in their total value as compared with the preceding year. The global quota for each product, however, shall be increased by not less than 10 per cent.

The quotas shall be increased annually in accordance with the same rules and in the same proportions in relation to the preceding year.

The fourth increase shall take place at the end of the fourth year after the entry into force of this Treaty; the fifth, one year after the beginning of the second stage. . . .

Article 34

1. Quantitative restrictions on exports, and all measures having equivalent effect, shall be prohibited between Member States.

2. Member States shall, by the end of the first stage at the latest, abolish all quantitative restrictions on exports and any measures

having equivalent effect which are in existence when this Treaty enters into force.

Article 35

The Member States declare their readiness to abolish quantitative restrictions on imports from and exports to other Member States more rapidly than is provided for in the preceding Articles, if their general economic situation and the situation of the economic sector concerned so permit.

To this end, the Commission shall make recommendations to the States concerned.

Article 36

The provisions of Articles 30 to 34 shall not preclude prohibitions or restrictions on imports, exports or goods in transit justified on grounds of public morality, public policy or public security; the protection of health and life of humans, animals or plants; the protection of national treasures possessing artistic, historic or archaeological value; or the protection of industrial and commercial property. Such prohibitions or restrictions shall not, however, constitute a means of arbitrary discrimination or a disguised restriction on trade between Member States. . . .

AGRICULTURE

Article 38

1. The common market shall extend to agriculture and trade in agricultural products. 'Agricultural products' means the products of the soil, of stock-farming and of fisheries and products of first-stage processing directly related to these products.

2. Save as otherwise provided in Articles 39 to 46, the rules laid down for the establishment of the common market shall apply to agricultural products.

3. The products subject to the provisions of Articles 39 to 46 are listed in Annex II to this Treaty. Within two years of the entry into force of this Treaty, however, the Council shall, acting by a qualified majority on a proposal from the Commission, decide what products are to be added to this list.

4. The operation and development of the common market for agricultural products must be accompanied by the establishment of a common agricultural policy among the Member States.

Article 39

1. The objectives of the common agricultural policy shall be:

(a) to increase agricultural productivity by promoting technical progress and by ensuring the rational development of agricultural production and the optimum utilization of the factors of production, in particular labour;
(b) thus to ensure a fair standard of living for the agricultural community, in particular by increasing the individual earnings of persons engaged in agriculture;
(c) to stabilize markets;
(d) to assure the availability of supplies;
(e) to ensure that supplies reach consumers at reasonable prices.

2. In working out the common agricultural policy and the special methods for its application, account shall be taken of:

(a) the particular nature of agricultural activity, which results from the social structure of agriculture and from structural and natural disparities between the various agricultural regions;
(b) the need to effect the appropriate adjustments by degrees;
(c) the fact that in the Member States agriculture constitutes a sector closely linked with the economy as a whole.

Article 40

1. Member States shall develop the common agricultural policy by degrees during the transitional period and shall bring it into force by the end of that period at the latest.

2. In order to attain the objectives set out in Article 39 a common organization of agricultural markets shall be established.

This organization shall take one of the following forms, depending on the product concerned;

(a) common rules on competiton;
(b) compulsory coordination of the various national market organizations;
(c) a European market organization.

3. The common organization established in accordance with paragraph 2 may include all measures required to attain the objectives set out in Article 39, in particular regulation of prices, aids for the

production and marketing of the various products, storage and carry-over arrangements and common machinery for stabilizing imports or exports.

The common organization shall be limited to pursuit of the objectives set out in Article 39 and shall exclude any discrimination between producers or consumers within the Community.

Any common price policy shall be based on common criteria and uniform methods of calculation.

4. In order to enable the common organization referred to in paragraph 2 to attain its objectives, one or more agricultural guidance and guarantee funds may be set up. . . .

FREE MOVEMENT OF PERSONS, SERVICES AND CAPITAL

Article 48

1. Freedom of movement for workers shall be secured within the Community by the end of the transitional period at the latest.

2. Such freedom of movement shall entail the abolition of any discrimination based on nationality between workers of the Member States as regards employment, remuneration and other conditions of work and employment.

3. It shall entail the right, subject to limitations justified on grounds of public policy, public security or public health:

(a) to accept offers of employment actually made;
(b) to move freely within the territory of Member States for this purpose;
(c) to stay in a Member State for the purpose of employment in accordance with the provisions governing the employment of nationals of that State laid down by law, regulation or administrative action;
(d) to remain in the territory of a Member State after having been employed in that State, subject to conditions which shall be embodied in implementing regulations to be drawn up by the Commission.

4. The provisions of this Article shall not apply to employment in the public service. . . .

Article 52

Within the framework of the provisions set out below, restrictions on the freedom of establishment of nationals of a Member State in the

territory of another Member State shall be abolished by progressive
stages in the course of the transitional period. Such progressive
abolition shall also apply to restrictions on the setting up of agencies,
branches or subsidiaries by nationals of any Member State established
in the territory of any Member State.

Freedom of establishment shall include the right to take up and
pursue activities as self-employed persons and to set up and manage
undertakings, in particular companies or firms . . . under the
conditions laid down for its own nationals by the law of the country
where such establishment is effected. . . .

Article 68

1. Member States shall . . . be as liberal as possible in granting such
exchange authorizations as are still necessary after the entry into force
of this Treaty.

2. Where a Member State applies to the movements of capital
liberalized in accordance with the provisions of this Chapter the
domestic rules governing the capital market and the credit system, it
shall do so in a non-discriminatory manner. . . .

SOCIAL POLICY

Article 117

Member States agree upon the need to promote improved working
conditions and an improved standard of living for workers, so as to
make possible their harmonization while the improvement is being
maintained.

They believe that such a development will ensue not only from the
functioning of the common market, which will favour the
harmonization of social systems, but also from the procedures
provided for in this Treaty and from the approximation of provisions
laid down by law, regulation or administrative action.

Article 118

Without prejudice to the other provisions of this Treaty and in
conformity with its general objectives, the Commission shall have the
task of promoting close cooperation between Member States in the
social field, particularly in matters relating to:

—employment;
—labour law and working conditions;

—basic and advanced vocational training;

—social security;

—prevention of occupational accidents and diseases;

—occupational hygiene;

—the right of association, and collective bargaining between employers and workers.

To this end, the Commission shall act in close contact with Member States by making studies, delivering opinions and arranging consultations both on problems arising at national level and on those of concern to international organizations.

Before delivering the opinions provided for in this Article, the Commission shall consult the Economic and Social Committee. . . .

THE EUROPEAN INVESTMENT BANK

Article 129

A European Investment Bank is hereby established; it shall have legal personality.

The members of the European Investment Bank shall be the Member States.

The Statute of the European Investment Bank is laid down in a Protocol annexed to this Treaty.

Article 130

The task of the European Investment Bank shall be to contribute, by having recourse to the capital market and utilizing its own resources, to the balanced and steady development of the common market in the interest of the Community. For this purpose the Bank shall, operating on a non-profit-making basis, grant loans and give guarantees which facilitate the financing of the following projects in all sectors of the economy:

(a) projects for developing less developed regions;

(b) projects for modernizing or converting undertakings or for developing fresh activities called for by the progressive establishment of the common market, where these projects are of such a size or nature that they cannot be entirely financed by the various means available in the individual Member States;

(c) projects of common interest to several Member States which are of such a size or nature that they cannot be entirely financed by the various means available in the individual Member States.

ASSOCIATION OF THE OVERSEAS COUNTRIES AND TERRITORIES

Article 131

The Member States agree to associate with the Community the non-European countries and territories which have special relations with Belgium, France, Italy and the Netherlands. These countries and territories (hereinafter called the 'countries and territories') are listed in Annex IV to this Treaty.

The purpose of association shall be to promote the economic and social development of the countries and territories and to establish close economic relations between them and the Community as a whole.

In accordance with the principles set out in the Preamble to this Treaty, association shall serve primarily to further the interests and prosperity of the inhabitants of these countries and territories in order to lead them to the economic, social and cultural development to which they aspire. . . .

THE INSTITUTIONS

Article 137

The Assembly, which shall consist of representatives of the peoples of the States brought together in the Community, shall exercise the advisory and supervisory powers which are conferred upon it by this Treaty.

Article 138

1. The Assembly shall consist of delegates who shall be designated by the respective Parliaments from among their members in accordance with the procedure laid down by each Member State.

2. The number of these delegates shall be as follows:

Belgium	14
Germany	36
France	36
Italy	36
Luxembourg	6
Netherlands	14

3. The Assembly shall draw up proposals for elections by direct universal suffrage in accordance with a uniform procedure in all Member States.

The Council shall, acting unanimously, lay down the appropriate provisions which it shall recommend to Member States for adoption in accordance with their respective constitutional requirements.

Article 139

The Assembly shall hold an annual session. It shall meet, without requiring to be convened, on the third Tuesday in October.

The Assembly may meet in extraordinary session at the request of a majority of its members or at the request of the Council or of the Commission. . . .

Article 143

The Assembly shall discuss in open session the annual general report submitted to it by the Commission.

Article 144

If a motion of censure on the activities of the Commission is tabled before it, the Assembly shall not vote thereon until at least three days after the motion has been tabled and only by open vote.

If the motion of censure is carried by a two-thirds majority of the votes cast, representing a majority of the members of the Assembly, the members of the Commission shall resign as a body. . . .

Article 145

To ensure that the objectives set out in this Treaty are attained, the Council shall, in accordance with the provisions of this Treaty:

—ensure coordination of the general economic policies of the Member States;
—have power to take decisions.

Article 146

The Council shall consist of representatives of the Member States. Each Government shall delegate to it one of its members.

The office of President shall be held for a term of six months by each member of the Council in turn, in the alphabetical order of the Member States.

Article *147*

The Council shall meet when convened by its President on his own initiative or at the request of one of its members or of the Commission.

Article *148*

1. Save as otherwise provided in this Treaty, the Council shall act by a majority of its members.

2. Where the Council is required to act by a qualified majority, the votes of its members shall be weighted as follows:

Belgium	2
Germany	4
France	4
Italy	4
Luxembourg	1
Netherlands	2

For their adoption, acts of the Council shall require at least:

—twelve votes in favour where this Treaty requires them to be adopted on a proposal from the Commission,

—twelve votes in favour, cast by at least four members, in other cases.

3. Abstentions by members present in person or represented shall not prevent the adoption by the Council of acts which require unanimity.

Article *149*

Where, in pursuance of this Treaty, the Council acts on a proposal from the Commission, unanimity shall be required for an act constituting an amendment to that proposal.

As long as the Council has not acted, the Commission may alter its original proposal, in particular where the Assembly has been consulted on that proposal.

Article *150*

Where a vote is taken, any member of the Council may also act on behalf of not more than one other member. . . .

Article 155

In order to ensure the proper functioning and development of the common market, the Commission shall:

—ensure that the provisions of this Treaty and the measures taken by the institutions pursuant thereto are applied;
—formulate recommendations or deliver opinions on matters dealt with in this Treaty, if it expressly so provides or if the Commission considers it necessary.
—have its own power of decision and participate in the shaping of measures taken by the Council and by the Assembly in the manner provided for in this Treaty;
—exercise the powers conferred on it by the Council for the implementation of the rules laid down by the latter.

Article 156

The Commission shall publish annually, not later than one month before the opening of the session of the Assembly, a general report on the activities of the Community.

Article 157

1. The Commission shall consist of nine members, who shall be chosen on the grounds of their general competence and whose independence is beyond doubt.

The number of members of the Commission may be altered by the Council, acting unanimously.

Only nationals of Member States may be members of the Commission.

The Commission may not include more than two members having the nationality of the same State.

2. The members of the Commission shall, in the general interest of the Community, be completely independent in the performance of their duties.

In the performance of these duties, they shall neither seek nor take instructions from any Government or from any other body. They shall refrain from any action incompatible with their duties. Each Member State undertakes to respect this principle and not to seek to influence the members of the Commission in the performance of their tasks.

The Members of the Commission may not, during their term of office, engage in any other occupation, whether gainful or not. When entering upon their duties they shall give a solemn undertaking that, both during and after their term of office, they will respect the obligations arising therefrom and in particular their duty to behave with integrity and discretion as regards the acceptance, after they have ceased to hold office, of certain appointments or benefits. In the event of any breach of these obligations, the Court of Justice may, on application by the Council or the Commission, rule that the member concerned be, according to the circumstances, either compulsorily retired . . . or deprived of his right to a pension or other benefits in its stead.

Article 158

The members of the Commission shall be appointed by common accord of the Governments of the Member States.

Their term of office shall be four years. It shall be renewable. . . .

Article 162

The Council and the Commission shall consult each other and shall settle by common accord their methods of cooperation.

The Commission shall adopt its rules of procedure so as to ensure that both it and its departments operate in accordance with the provisions of this Treaty. It shall ensure that these rules of procedure are published.

Article 163

The Commission shall act by a majority of the number of members provided for in Article 157.

A meeting of the Commission shall be valid only if the number of members laid down in its rules of procedure is present.

Article 164

The Court of Justice shall ensure that in the interpretation and application of this Treaty the law is observed.

Article 165

The Court of Justice shall consist of seven Judges.

The Court of Justice shall sit in plenary session. It may, however, form chambers, each consisting of three or five Judges, either to undertake certain preparatory inquiries or to adjudicate on particular categories of cases in accordance with rules laid down for these purposes. . . .

Article 189

In order to carry out their task the Council and the Commission shall, in accordance with the provisions of this Treaty, make regulations, issue directives, take decisions, make recommendations or deliver opinions.

A regulation shall have general application. It shall be binding in its entirety and directly applicable in all Member States.

A directive shall be binding, as to the result to be achieved, upon each Member State to which it is addressed, but shall leave to the national authorities the choice of form and methods.

A decision shall be binding in its entirety upon those to whom it is addressed.

Recommendations and opinions shall have no binding force. . . .

Article 191

Regulations shall be published in the Official Journal of the Community. They shall enter into force on the date specified in them or, in the absence thereof, on the twentieth day following their publication.

Directives and decisions shall be notified to those to whom they are addressed and shall take effect upon such notification. . . .

Article 193

An Economic and Social Committee is hereby established. It shall have advisory status.

The Committee shall consist of representatives of the various categories of economic and social activity, in particular, representatives of producers, farmers, carriers, workers, dealers, craftsmen, professional occupations and representatives of the general public.

The Members of the Committee shall be appointed by the Council, acting unanimously, for four years. Their appointments shall be renewable.

The members of the Committee shall be appointed in their personal capacity and may not be bound by any mandatory instructions. . . .

Article 237

Any European State may apply to become a member of the ,Community. It shall address its application to the Council, which shall act unanimously after obtaining the opinion of the Commission.

The conditions of admission and the adjustments to this Treaty necessitated thereby shall be the subject of an agreement between the Member States and the applicant State. This agreement shall be submitted for ratification by all the contracting States in accordance with their respective constitutional requirements. . . .

Article 240

This Treaty is concluded for an unlimited period.

Cmnd. 4864. London, HMSO

IV

Benelux, Norden and EFTA

In this and the next chapter we are reminded that the Six are not by any means the only countries to have been involved in post-war European integration, and that, even among them, economic integration has not been confined to the Common Market. Indeed, future historians may well date the origins of European integration from the foundation of Belux, the so-called Economic Union between Belgium and Luxembourg, established in 1922 (22). In some respects this was the forerunner of the later arrangements between these two countries and the Netherlands. We omit here the London Monetary Agreement between the Benelux powers, of 21 October, 1943, but we have included the Customs Convention signed in London on 5 September 1944 (18). Almost insuperable difficulties, mainly economic in nature, emerged at the end of the war to slow down the implementation of this apparently uncomplicated vision of the Dutch, Belgian and Luxembourg governments. Although 95 per cent of internal trade had been freed and the free movement of labour permitted by 1956, it was not until 1958 (20) that the Benelux Economic Union was finally set up. Even then, it was sadly incomplete, agricultural products, for example, being largely omitted. But it remains true that Benelux acted historically as a model, or inspiration, for the European Communities. The Three paved the way for the Six.

Very different from the three small, contiguous, densely populated Benelux states are the Scandinavian countries: vast, underpopulated, but (Finland apart) linguistically and culturally alike, with a centuries-long history of political or dynastic unions. Here, passports really are a thing of the past and legislative harmonization between States has in some fields progressed further even than in the United States of America. Yet Norway, Denmark, Sweden and Finland have set up no common supranational institutions. Alongside persistent and widespread 'Scandinavianism' one finds intense nationalism. Each country has often preferred to go its own way:

Denmark into the EEC but not Norway; Norway into NATO but not Sweden. Long ago, in 1952, these countries set up the Nordic Council (19), but this is only an advisory and coordinatory inter-governmental and interparliamentary institution. It has a Statute but forms no part of the law or constitution of its Member States. Thus, in spite of the Nordic Council, in spite of the pious aspirations of the 1962 Treaty of Cooperation renewed in 1971, and the Council of Ministers it set up (23), Norden does not yet exist. The sort of form it might have begun to take is perhaps shown in the draft treaty establishing Nordek, which provided for a Nordic Customs Union (24); this was drawn up in 1969 but never implemented.

In this section the EFTA Treaty (21) is in a sense the odd man out. Yet it is, of course, in some ways Scandinavian in character and was brought about partly through Scandinavian initiatives. The creation of the Seven should by no means be regarded as a rather silly counter-ploy to the Six, even though efforts were made to put pressure on the Six. There was nothing essentially divisive in the attempts made by all the member states of the OEEC, in 1956–1959, to find some way of creating a free trade area which would include all the OEEC members, that is, the whole of Western Europe, and incorporate the Common Market of the Six. But, just as a customs union has unquestioned economic benefits to confer on a group of contiguous countries with economies more or less complementary; so a free trade area seemed the natural thing for the widely spaced OEEC countries whose firm policies of neutrality (Austria, Switzerland, Sweden) or some other special reason (to a large extent the Commonwealth in Britain's case) had caused to be, as it were, 'left out' of the Common Market.

18 Customs Convention between the Netherlands and the Economic Union of Belgium and Luxembourg, London, 5 September 1944, with 1947 Protocol amendments

The Government of Her Majesty the Queen of the Netherlands on the one hand;
The Government of His Majesty the King of the Belgians and of Her Royal Highness the Grand Duchess of Luxembourg on the other hand,
Desiring at the moment of liberation [from German occupation] of the Territories of the Netherlands and the Economic Union of Belgium and Luxembourg, to create the most favourable conditions for the

ultimate formation of an Economic Union and for the restoration of
economic activity, have decided to further these ends by establishing a
system of common duties and to this end have agreed to the following
articles:

Article 1

The Netherlands and the Economic Union of Belgium and
Luxembourg shall impose identical customs duties on the importation
of goods, according to the appended tariff which forms an integral
part of this agreement.

Apart from the duties provided for in this tariff, they shall be
entitled to levy excise duties—including import duties equivalent to
excise—as well as any other dues, according to the system in force in
their respective Territories; they shall reserve the right to modify the
rates.

Article 2

No customs duty shall be levied on goods entering the Netherlands
from the Economic Union of Belgium and Luxembourg and
reciprocally on goods entering the Economic Union of Belgium and
Luxembourg from the Netherlands.

The Netherlands and the Economic Union of Belgium and
Luxembourg shall be entitled to levy entry duties—including import
duties equivalent to excise—as well as any other taxes, according to the
system in force in their respective territories; they reserve their right to
modify the rates.

Article 3

An Administrative Council on Customs Duties shall be constituted;
this shall be composed of three delegates of the Netherlands and three
delegates of the Economic Union of Belgium and Luxembourg. The
chairmanship of the Administrative Council on Customs Duties shall
be exercised in turn by the first delegate of the Netherlands and the
first delegate of the Economic Union of Belgium and Luxembourg.

The Administrative Council on Customs Duties shall propose
measures aimed at the unification of the legislative provisions and
regulations governing the collection of import and excise duties in the
Netherlands and in the Economic Union of Belgium and Luxembourg
and the adjustment of the latter to the provisions of this agreement
without prejudice to the preliminary provisions of the annexed tariff.

Article 4

The Administrative Council on Customs Duties shall be assisted by a Commission on Customs Disputes, composed of two delegates of the Netherlands and two delegates of the Economic Union of Belgium and Luxembourg.

The Commission on Customs Disputes, at the request of the competent ministers, shall make a binding award in the case of disputes arising from the application of the legal provisions and regulations resulting from this agreement.

The Commission shall communicate its decisions to the competent ministers, who shall be responsible for carrying them out within the limits of their respective competence.

Article 5

A Council for the Economic Union shall be constituted, composed of three delegates of the Netherlands and three delegates of the Economic Union of Belgium and Luxembourg. The chairmanship of the Council of the Economic Union shall be exercised in turn by the first delegate of the Netherlands and the first delegate of the Economic Union of Belgium and Luxembourg.

The functions of the Council for the Economic Union shall be:

(a) giving its views to the competent authorities in the Netherlands and the Economic Union of Belgium and Luxembourg concerning any measures which they might intend to take for the purpose of regulating imports, exports and transit either with or without accessory duties or dues in particular by imposing restrictions of an economic character, such as licences, quotas, or special licence fees and administrative charges;

(b) coordinating the above measures for the purpose of establishing a regime common to the Netherlands and the Economic Union of Belgium and Luxembourg;

(c) administering the import, export and transit quotas common to the Netherlands and the Economic Union of Belgium and Luxembourg;

(d) informing the competent authorities in the Netherlands and the Economic Union of Belgium and Luxembourg of its views concerning all measures relating to production bounties or subsidies which the Contracting Parties intend to take.

Article 6

A Commercial Agreements Council shall be constituted, composed of three delegates of the Netherlands and three delegates of the Economic Union of Belgium and Luxembourg. The chairmanship of the Commercial Agreements Council shall be exercised in turn by the first delegate of the Netherlands and by the first delegate of the Economic Union of Belgium and Luxembourg.

The Commercial Agreements Council shall whenever possible ensure the coördination of measures in respect of relations established with third States.

Article 7

The joint measures mentioned under Articles 3, 5 and 6 of this Agreement shall be decided upon by the competent ministers on behalf of the Netherlands on the one hand and of the Economic Union of Belgium and Luxembourg on the other and shall be referred to the competent governmental or legal authorities for approval.

Article 8

The present Convention shall be ratified and shall come into force on the first day of the third month after the instruments of ratification have been exchanged. It may be cancelled at any time provided that one year's notice is given.

It shall in any case cease to be operative on the implementation of the long-term Economic Union which the contracting Parties intend to conclude.

Article 9

Pending the exchange of instruments of ratification, the Convention shall come into force as soon as the Netherlands and Belgian Governments reintegrate their respective territories.

Either Government however shall have the right to cancel the Convention at any time provided that six months notice is given.

In witness whereof, the Ministers Plenipotentiary, provided with the necessary powers to this end, have signed the present Convention and fixed their seals thereto.

European Yearbook 2: 283–7. The Hague, 1956

19   The Nordic Council Statute of 1952

Article 1

Det nordiske Rad (The Nordic Council) is a body formed for the purpose of consultation among the Rigsdag of Denmark, the Althing of Iceland, the Storting of Norway and the Riksdag of Sweden and the Governments of Denmark, Iceland, Norway and Sweden in matters involving joint action by any or all of these countries.

Article 2

The Council shall consist of sixteen delegates from each of the legislative assemblies of Denmark, Norway and Sweden, and the requisite numbers of deputy delegates, representing different political opinions, elected by the aforesaid legislative assemblies from amongst their members, for such periods and by such methods as shall be decided in each country. The legislative assembly of Iceland shall elect five delegates according to similar rules.

The Governments of the participating countries shall be represented on the Council by such of their members as shall be appointed by them for each particular case.

The Government representatives take part in the deliberations of the Council, but not in its decisions.

Article 3

Upon a request by Finland, Finnish Representatives may take part in the deliberations and decisions of the Council.

Article 4

The Council shall meet once a year on such date as it may decide (Ordinary Session). Further, the Council will meet when it so decides or when a meeting is requested by not less than two Governments or not less than twenty delegates (Extraordinary Session). Sessions shall be held in the capitals of the respective countries, as decided by the Council.

Article 5

For each session and the time up to the following session, the Council shall elect one President and three Deputy Presidents who together shall constitute the Praesidium of the Council.

Article 6

The deliberations of the Council shall be open to the public unless, in view of the special nature of a matter, the Council decides otherwise.

Article 7

The requisite number of committees shall be set up to undertake preparatory work in connection with matters before the Council. Committees may meet also during inter-sessionary periods whenever the Council so decides.

Article 8

The delegation of each country shall appoint a Secretary and other staff members. The activities and mutual collaboration of the secretariats shall be supervised by the Praesidium.

Article 9

Each Government and each delegate have the right to submit a matter to the Council. Unless the Council decides otherwise, such matters shall be transmitted to the Praesidium through the national Secretariat concerned and forwarded to the delegates in good time before the next session, together with such explanatory reports as the Praesidium may deem necessary.

Article 10

The task of the Council is to discuss questions of common interest to the countries and to adopt recommendations to the Governments on such questions. Such recommendations shall be accompanied by information as to how each delegate has voted.

In deliberations on questions which do not concern all of the member Countries, only the representatives of the countries concerned may take part in the decisions of the Council.

The Council shall decide on its own organization and on the activities of the Secretariats.

Article 11

In each Ordinary Session, the Governments should submit information on the action taken on the recommendations of the Council.

Article 12

The Council shall adopt its own rules of procedure.

Article 13

Each country shall defray the expenses of its own representation and national Secretariat and also the extraordinary expenses involved by sessions held in its territory. Common expenses shall be defrayed in accordance with the decision of the Council.

Article 14

This Statute shall enter into force as soon as similar statutes have been adopted in Norway and Sweden. The date and place of the first Session of the Council will then be agreed upon without delay.

Article 15

This Statute shall enter into force in relation to Iceland as soon as a similar Statute has been adopted by that country.

A. H. Robertson, *European Institutions*, 469–71, London, 1973

20 Treaty Instituting the Benelux Economic Union, 3 February 1958

His Majesty the King of the Belgians,
Her Royal Highness the Grand Duchess of Luxembourg,
Her Majesty the Queen of the Netherlands,

Being resolved to strengthen the economic ties between their countries by means of free movement of persons, goods, capital and services;

Desiring to coordinate their policies in the economic, financial and social fields in order to attain the most satisfactory level of employment and the highest standard of living in keeping with economic circumstances and compatible with the maintenance of monetary stability;

Desiring to pursue a joint trade policy directed towards the most favourable development of the exchange of goods and services with third countries by means of the freest possible trade;

Believing that economic progress, forming the principal aim of their union, must lead to the advancement of the individual and social welfare of their peoples;

Noting that, by virtue of Article 233 of the Treaty establishing the

EEC and Article 202 of the Treaty establishing the Euratom, signed at Rome on the twenty-fifth day of March, 1957, those Treaties do not preclude the existence or creation of an Economic Union between their countries in so far as the objects of this Union are not attained by the application of the said Treaties,

Having decided to establish the Economic Union between their countries as envisaged by the Customs Convention signed in London on 5 September 1944, defined and interpreted in accordance with the Protocol signed at The Hague on 14 March 1947,

Have thereto appointed as their plenipotentiaries: [*names follow*].

Article 1

1. An Economic Union is established between the Kingdom of Belgium, the Grand Duchy of Luxembourg and the Kingdom of the Netherlands, entailing free movement of persons, goods, capital and services.

2. This Union implies:

(*a*) the coordination of economic, financial and social policies;

(*b*) the pursuit of a joint policy in economic relations with third countries and regarding payments related thereto.

Article 2

1. The nationals of each High Contracting Party may freely enter and leave the territory of any other Contracting Party.

2. They shall enjoy the same treatment as nationals of that State as regards:

(*a*) freedom of movement, sojourn and settlement;

(*b*) freedom to carry on a trade or occupation, including the rendering of services;

(*c*) capital transactions;

(*d*) conditions of employment;

(*e*) social security benefits;

(*f*) taxes and charges of any kind;

(*g*) exercise of civil rights as well as legal and judicial protection of their person, individual rights and interests.

Article 3

1. Goods traffic between the territories of the High Contracting Parties, irrespective of origin, last exporting country or destination of the goods, shall be free of import and excise duty and any other duties, charges, imposts or dues of whatsoever kind.

2. It shall likewise be free from all prohibitions or restrictions of an economic or financial nature, such as quotas, restrictions applying to certain types of goods or currency restrictions.

3. Goods originating from the territory of one of the High Contracting Parties shall receive in the territories of the other Contracting Parties the same treatment as national products. . . .

Article 8

1. The High Contracting Parties shall, in close consultation, pursue a coordinated policy in the economic, financial and social fields.

2. The High Contracting Parties shall coordinate their policies in respect of private commercial agreements and of abuses arising from the dominant position of one or more concerns; they shall take steps to prevent the abuse of economic power. . . .

Article 10

In their relations with third countries the High Contracting Parties shall:

(a) accept and pursue a joint policy in the field of foreign trade and of payments related thereto;

(b) jointly conclude treaties and conventions regarding foreign trade and the customs tariff;

(c) conclude, either jointly or concurrently, treaties and conventions regarding payments in connection with foreign trade.

Article 11

1. As regards goods coming from or destined for third countries, import duties and excise duties as well as all other taxes, imposts or dues whatsoever, to be imposed on account of imports, exports or transit traffic, shall be fixed in accordance with a common tariff with identical rates, the regulations for levying the same being coordinated.

2. The procedure in the matter of licenses and quotas with regard to imports, exports and transit shall be identical.

3. The High Contracting Parties shall coordinate all regulations, either legal or executive, and other stipulations of public law of an economic or financial nature regarding imports, exports or transit traffic, which are not covered by the first and second paragraphs of this Article.

Article 12

1. As regards the rate of exchange between the Netherlands guilder and the Belgian and the Luxembourg franc, the High Contracting Parties shall determine their policies by mutual agreement. Likewise, by mutual agreement they shall fix their exchange rates in relation to the currencies of third countries.

2. In particular they shall not effect any alteration of rates of exchange except by mutual agreement. . . .

Article 15

The institutions of the Union shall consist of:
(a) the Committee of Ministers;
(b) the Consultative Interparliamentary Council;
(c) the Council of the Economic Union;
(d) the Committees and the Special Committees;
(e) the General Secretariat;
(f) Joint Services;
(g) the College of Arbitrators;
(h) the Economic and Social Advisory Council.

Article 16

The Committee of Ministers shall see to the application of this Treaty and ensure the realization of the aims covered thereby. It shall institute any measures required for these purposes, in accordance with the provisions of the present Treaty.

Article 17

1. Each High Contracting Party shall appoint at least three members of its Government to sit on the Committee.

2. Each Government may invite other members to take part in a particular session, whenever it so desires.

Article 18

The Committee shall take decisions unanimously. Each High Contracting Party shall have one vote. The abstention of one High Contracting Party shall not prevent a decision being taken. . . .

Article 20

1. The Committee of Ministers shall meet at least once every three months. In an emergency it shall assemble at the request of the Government of any one of the High Contracting Parties.

2. For each successive period of six months the Chair will be taken in rotation by a Belgian, Luxembourg or Netherlands member, irrespective of the place of meeting. . . .

Article 25

The Council of the Economic Union shall be responsible for:

(a) coordinating the activities of Committees and Special Committees. To this end it may issue any directives required. Proposals from Committees and Special Committees will be forwarded by the Council to the Committee of Ministers together with its opinion, if required;

(b) carrying into effect decisions of the Committee of Ministers as far as the Council is concerned;

(c) submitting proposals to the Committee of Ministers which it may deem advantageous for the functioning of the Union. . . .

Article 33

The seat of the Secretariat General shall be established at Brussels. . . .

Article 35

1. The members of the staff shall be of Belgian, Luxembourg or Netherlands nationality. . . .

Article 41

The College of Arbitrators shall be entrusted with the task of settling such disputes as may arise between the High Contracting Parties with regard to the application of the present Treaty and of Conventions related to the aims of this Treaty. . . .

Article 72

1. The Committee of Ministers shall determine a joint trade policy in economic relations with third countries and shall establish measures for its application.

2. In particular, the Committee will fix joint import and export quotas. . . .

Article 94

1. The provisions of the present Treaty shall not be contrary to the existence or possible development of the Economic Union between the Kingdom of Belgium and the Grand Duchy of Luxembourg insofar as the objectives of that Union are not attained by the application of the present Treaty.

2. The Belgian and Luxembourg Governments shall examine the aggregate of treaties and conventions constituting the Economic Union between these countries; prior to establishing provisions on which they agree, these countries will inform the Netherlands Government of the result of this examination. . . .

Article 96

The official languages of the institutions of the Union shall be the Netherlands and French languages. . . .

Article 99

1. The present Treaty shall be concluded for a period of fifty years.

2. Thereafter the Treaty remains operative for consecutive periods of ten years unless one of the High Contracting Parties notifies the other Contracting Parties one year before the expiration of the current period of its intention to terminate the present Treaty.

Unofficial translation supplied by the
Secretariat General of Benelux

21   Convention of Stockholm establishing the EFTA, 4 January 1960, with amendments to 1973

The Republic of Austria, the Kingdom of Denmark, the Kingdom of Norway, the Portuguese Republic, the Kingdom of Sweden, the Swiss Confederation and the United Kingdom of Great Britain and Northern Ireland:[1]

Having regard to the Convention for European Economic Cooperation of 16 April 1948, which established the OEEC;

Resolved to maintain and develop the cooperation instituted within that Organization;

[1] Iceland acceded to the Convention on 1 March 1970; Denmark and the United Kingdom withdrew from the Convention on 1 January 1973.

Determined to facilitate the early establishment of a multilateral association for the removal of trade barriers and the promotion of closer economic cooperation between the Members of the OEEC, including the Members of the EEC;

Having regard to the General Agreement on Tariffs and Trade;

Resolved to promote the objectives of that Agreement;

Have agreed as follows:

Article 1: The Association

1. An international organization to be known as the European Free Trade Association, hereinafter referred to as 'the Association', is hereby established. . . .

4. The Institutions of the Association shall be a Council and such other organs as the Council may set up.

Article 2: Objectives

The objectives of the Association shall be

(a) to promote in the Area of the Association and in each Member State a sustained expansion of economic activity, full employment, increased productivity and the rational use of resources, financial stability and continuous improvement in living standards,

(b) to secure that trade between Member States takes place in conditions of fair competition,

(c) to avoid significant disparity between Member States in the conditions of supply of raw materials produced within the Area of the Association, and

(d) to contribute to the harmonious development and expansion of world trade and to the progressive removal of barriers to it.

Article 3: Import duties

1. Member States shall reduce and ultimately eliminate, in accordance with this Article, customs duties and any other charges with equivalent effect, except duties notified in accordance with Article 6 and other charges which fall within that Article, imposed on or in connection with the importation of goods which are eligible for Area tariff treatment in accordance with Article 4. Any such duty or other charge is hereinafter referred to as an 'import duty'.

2. (a) On and after each of the following dates, Member States shall not apply an import duty on any product at a level exceeding the percentage of the basic duty specified against that date:

1 July	1960	80 per cent
1 July	1961	70 per cent
1 March	1962	60 per cent
31 October	1962	50 per cent
31 December	1963	40 per cent
31 December	1964	30 per cent
31 December	1965	20 per cent

(*b*) On and after 31 December 1966,[1] Member States shall not apply any import duties.

3. Subject to Annex A, the basic duty referred to in paragraph 2 of this Article is, in respect of each Member State and in respect of any product, the import duty applied by that Member State to the imports of that product from other Member States on 1 January 1960.

4. Each Member State declares its willingness to apply import duties at a level below that indicated in paragraph 2 of this Article if it considers that its economic and financial position and the position of the sector concerned so permit.

5. The Council may at any time decide that any import duties shall be reduced more rapidly or eliminated earlier than is provided in paragraph 2 of this Article. Between 1 July 1960 and 31 December 1961 the Council shall examine whether it is possible so to decide in respect of import duties applied on some or all goods by some or all of the Member States.

Article 4: Area tariff treatment

1. For the purposes of this Convention goods shall be accepted as eligible for Area tariff treatment if they are originating products in accordance with the provisions of Annex B.

2. Provisions necessary for the administration and effective application of this Article are contained in Annex B and Council Decisions.

3. Nothing in this Convention shall prevent a Member State from accepting as eligible for Area tariff treatment any goods imported from the territory of another Member State, provided that the like goods imported from the territory of any Member State are accorded the same treatment.

4. The Council shall from time to time examine in what respect this Convention can be amended in order to ensure the smooth operation of the origin rules and especially to make them simpler and more liberal. . . .

[1] This and the preceding six dates are all as amended in 1961–3 by Council decision.

Article 6: Revenue duties and internal taxation

1. Member States shall not

(a) apply directly or indirectly to imported goods any fiscal charges in excess of those applied directly or indirectly to like domestic goods, nor otherwise apply such charges so as to afford effective protection to like domestic goods, or

(b) apply fiscal charges to imported goods of a kind which they do not produce, or which they do not produce in substantial quantities, in such a way as to afford effective protection to the domestic production of goods of a different kind which are substitutable for the imported goods, which enter into direct competition with them and which do not bear directly or indirectly, in the country of importation, fiscal charges of equivalent incidence. . . .

Article 8: Prohibition of export duties

1. Member States shall not introduce or increase export duties, and, on and after 1 January 1962, shall not apply any such duties. . . .

Article 10: Quantitative import restrictions

1. Member States shall not introduce or intensify quantitative restrictions on imports of goods from the territory of other Member States.

2. Member States shall eliminate such quantitative restrictions as soon as possible and not later than 31 December 1966. . . .

Article 13: Government aids

1. Member States shall not maintain or introduce

(a) the forms of aid to exports of goods to other Member States which are described in Annex C, or

(b) any other form of aid, the main purpose or effect of which is to frustrate the benefits expected from the removal or absence of duties and quantitative restrictions on trade between Member States. . . .

Article 19: Balance of payments difficulties

1. Notwithstanding the provisions of Article 10, any Member State may, consistently with its other international obligations, introduce quantitative restrictions on imports for the purpose of safeguarding its balance of payments. . . .

Article 22: Agricultural policies and objective

1. In regard to agriculture, Member States recognize that the policies pursued by them are designed

(a) to promote increased productivity and the rational and economic development of production,

(b) to provide a reasonable degree of market stability and adequate supplies to consumers at reasonable prices, and

(c) to ensure an adequate standard of living to persons engaged in agriculture.

In pursuing these policies, Member States shall have due regard to the interests of other Member States in the export of agricultural goods and shall take into consideration traditional channels of trade.

2. Having regard to these policies, the objective of the Association shall be to facilitate an expansion of trade which will provide reasonable reciprocity to Member States whose economies depend to a great extent on exports of agricultural goods. . . .

Article 32: The Council

1. It shall be the responsibility of the Council

(a) to exercise such powers and functions as are conferred upon it by this Convention,

(b) to supervise the application of this Convention and keep its operation under review, and

(c) to consider whether further action should be taken by Member States in order to promote the attainment of the objectives of the Association and to facilitate the establishment of closer links with other States, unions of States or international organizations.

2. Each Member State shall be represented in the Council and shall have one vote.

3. The Council may decide to set up such organs, committees and other bodies as it considers necessary to assist it in accomplishing its tasks.

4. In exercising its responsibility under paragraph 1 of this Article, the Council may take decisions which shall be binding on all Member States and may make recommendations to Member States.

5. Decisions and recommendations of the Council shall be made by unanimous vote, except in so far as this Convention provides otherwise. Decisions or recommendations shall be regarded as unanimous unless any Member State casts a negative vote. Decisions

and recommendations which are to be made by majority vote require the affirmative vote of four Member States.

6. If the number of the Member States changes, the Council may decide to amend the number of votes required for decisions and recommendations which are to be made by majority vote. . . .

Convention establishing the European Free Trade
Association, 6–37. EFTA, Geneva, July 1973

22 **Coordinated Convention establishing the Belgian-Luxembourgeoise Economic Union signed on 29 January 1963, as modified by the 27 October 1971 Protocol, continuing the Economic Union originally established on 6 March 1922**

Article 1

An Economic Union based on a customs union is hereby established between the Kingdom of Belgium and the Grand Duchy of Luxembourg.

Article 2

In so far as customs, excise duties common to both countries, and measures taken in common to regulate external trade are concerned, the territories of the High Contracting Parties shall be taken to form a single territory; the tariff frontier between the two countries is hereby suppressed.

Article 3

Apart from the exceptions provided for in the present Convention there shall be full and complete freedom of trade between the countries forming the Union, without any hindrances or prohibitions of imports, exports or the transit of goods, and without the levying of any kind of duties or taxes.

Article 4

The implementation of the provisions of this Convention shall be ensured by the following institutions, each of them acting within the framework of its attributions: a Committee of Ministers; an Administrative Commission; a Customs Council.

Article 5

The legal and prescribed regulations concerning customs duties shall be common to the Union as a whole.

Article 6

1. The Council of Ministers shall deal with the institution, the modification, and the suppression of common excise duties. . . .

2. Goods subject to a common excise duty may be sent from the territory of one of the High Contracting Parties to that of the other without the levying, restitution or rebate of the excise duties payable on either imports or exports.

3. Home-produced non-sparkling natural wines made with fresh grapes may not suffer any excise duty. As regards the application of the present Convention, wines made from grapes harvested in the Grand Duchy of Luxembourg in accordance with the laws of Luxembourg are considered home-produced natural wines.

Article 7

Apart from the attributions of the Customs Council, each of the two governments shall be responsible for the administration and levying of customs and excise duties on its own territory, in accordance with the laws and regulations of the customs union. . . .

Article 11

1. Each Member State of the Union shall recruit its customs and excise personnel exclusively from its own nationals.

2. The personnel of the Luxembourgeois customs shall adopt the uniform, cockade excepted, the equipment, and the arms of the Belgian customs service. . . .

Article 14

1. The Customs Council shall consist of three members, namely the director-general of the customs and excise of Belgium, to be president; the director of the Luxembourgeois customs; and a member nominated by the Belgian government from among its customs and excise officers having the rank of inspector-general.

2. The Customs Council's decisions are to be made unanimously. In the event of disagreement between the members, the question is to be referred to the Committee of Ministers. . . .

Article 16

The subjects of each of the High Contracting Parties shall enjoy in the territory of the other Contracting Party the same rights of passage and sojourn accorded to its own nationals; apart from any restrictions decided on by the Council of Ministers in the interests of law and order, security, and public health or morality.

Article 17

The subjects of each of the High Contracting Parties shall enjoy in the territory of the other Contracting Party the same civil rights as its own nationals, as well as the same legal and juridical protection of their persons, rights and interests.

Article 18

As far as access to and the exercise of independent economic activity is concerned, the subjects of each of the High Contracting Parties shall be treated in the territory of the other Contracting Party in the same way as its own nationals. . . .

Article 23

1. With a view to promoting the proper functioning of the Union set up by the present Convention, the High Contracting parties shall:

—pursue, in close mutual consultation, coordinated economic, financial and social policies;

—aim for the harmonization of legal, statutary and administrative regulations which bear directly on the functioning of the Union;

—together see to it that no law or administrative regulation unduly hinders trade between the two countries;

—make an effort to eliminate any disparities between the legal, statutary and administrative regulations which might upset free competition between the markets of the two countries;

—help each other to ensure that the measures of political economy taken in each of the two countries are efficacious.

Article 24

The two countries must be placed on a footing of perfect equality in the supply of combustibles, of energy and of raw materials.

Article 25

1. The governments of the High Contracting Parties shall pursue a coordinated policy as regards prices. . . .

Article 36

1. The Committee of Ministers shall consist of members of the two governments.

2. The task of the Committee of Ministers is to take the decisions necessary for the proper functioning of the Union; to concert the common legal and administrative measures laid down in this Convention; and to discuss questions concerning external economic relations.

3. The Committee of Ministers shall act by the mutual agreement of the Belgian and Luxembourgeois Ministers present.

Article 37

1. The Administrative Commission shall be composed of the delegates of the two governments.

2. The task of the Administrative Commission is to see to the implementation of the present Convention and to ensure, to this effect, a regular liaison between the two governments. It will make proposals for submission to the Committee of Ministers. . . .

Article 43

The present Convention has been concluded for a period of fifty years starting on 6 March 1922. It will remain in force for successive periods of ten years. . . .[1]

> Editor's translation from French text
> supplied by the Benelux Secretariat General

23 Treaty of Cooperation between Denmark, Finland, Iceland, Norway and Sweden, signed in Helsinki on 23 March 1962, as amended on 13 February 1971

Preamble to the Treaty of Cooperation of 23 March 1962

The Governments of Denmark, Finland, Iceland, Norway and Sweden,

Desirous of furthering the close connections between the Nordic nations in culture and in juridical and social conceptions and of developing cooperation between the Nordic countries;

Endeavouring to create uniform rules in the Nordic countries in as many respects as possible;

Hoping to achieve in all fields where prerequisites exist an appropriate division of labour between these countries;

Desirous of continuing the cooperation, important to these countries, in the Nordic Council and other agencies of cooperation;

Have agreed upon the following provisions.

[1] On 1 March 1971 the Union was prolonged for a further ten years from 6 March 1972.

Preamble to the agreement of 13 February 1971

The Governments of Denmark, Finland, Iceland, Norway and Sweden, desirous of strengthening and further enlarging the institutional foundations of the cooperation between the Nordic countries,

Considering it appropriate for this purpose to amend the Treaty of Cooperation of 23 March 1962, between the Nordic countries,

Having therefore decided to include in the Treaty of Cooperation the fundamental provisions regarding the Nordic Council,

Having also decided to include in the Treaty of Cooperation provisions regarding a Nordic Council of Ministers, with competence in the whole field of Nordic cooperation,

Have agreed as follows

ARTICLES OF THE 1962 TREATY

Article 1

The Contracting Parties shall endeavour to maintain and further develop cooperation between the countries in the juridical, cultural, social and economic fields and in questions of transport and communications.

Article 2

The Contracting Parties shall continue the work to attain the highest possible degree of juridical equality between a national of any Nordic country, resident in a Nordic country other than his own, and the citizens of his country of residence.

Article 3

The Contracting Parties shall endeavour to facilitate the acquisition of citizenship by nationals of one Nordic country in another Nordic country.

Article 4

The Contracting Parties shall continue legislative cooperation in order to attain the greatest possible uniformity in Private Law.

Article 5

The Contracting Parties should strive to create uniform provisions regarding crime and the consequences of crime. . . .

Article 8

In each Nordic country, education and training given at school shall include, in a suitable degree, instruction in the language, culture and general social conditions of the other Nordic countries.

Article 9

Each Contracting Party should maintain and extend the opportunities for a student from another Nordic country to pursue studies and graduate in its educational establishments. It should also be possible to the greatest possible extent to count a part examination passed in any Nordic country towards a final examination taken in another Nordic country.

It should be possible [for students] to receive economic assistance from their country of domicile, irrespective of the country where their studies are pursued.

Article 10

The Contracting Parties should coordinate public education qualifying for a given profession or trade.

Such education should, as far as possible, have the same qualifying value in all the Nordic countries. Additional studies necessary for reasons connected with national conditions can, however, be required. . . .

Article 12

Cooperation in the field of research should be so organized that research funds and other resources available will be coordinated and exploited in the best possible way, among other things by establishing joint institutions. . . .

Article 14

The Contracting Parties shall strive to preserve and further develop the common Nordic Labour Market along the lines drawn up in earlier agreements. Labour exchanges and vocational guidance shall be coordinated. The exchange of trainees shall be free.

Efforts should be made to achieve uniformity in national regulations on industrial safety and other questions of a similar nature.

Article 15

The Contracting Parties shall strive for arrangements whereby it will be possible for the nationals of one Nordic country, while staying in another Nordic country, to receive, as far as possible, the same social benefits as are offered to the citizens of the country of residence. . . .

Article 18

The Contracting Parties shall, in order to promote economic cooperation in different fields, consult one another on questions of economic policy. Attention shall be devoted to the possibilities of coordinating measures taken to level out cyclical fluctuations.

Article 19

The Contracting Parties intend, in so far as possible, to promote cooperation between their countries in production and investment, striving to create conditions for direct cooperation between enterprises in two or more Nordic countries. In the further development of international cooperation, the Contracting Parties should strive to achieve an appropriate division of labour between the countries in the fields of production and investment.

Article 20

The Contracting Parties shall work for the greatest possible freedom of capital movement between the Nordic countries. In other payments and currency questions of common interest joint solutions shall be sought.

Article 21

The Contracting Parties shall seek to consolidate the cooperation started earlier to remove barriers to trade between the Nordic countries and, to the greatest extent possible, to strengthen and further develop this cooperation.

Article 22

In issues of international commercial policy the Contracting Parties shall endeavour, both separately and jointly, to promote the interests of the Nordic countries and, with this purpose in view, to consult one another.

Article 23

The Contracting Parties shall strive for coordination of technical and administrative customs regulations and for simplification of customs procedure in order to facilitate communications between the countries. . . .

Article 26

The Contracting Parties shall seek to consolidate the earlier cooperation in the field of traffic and seek to develop this cooperation in order to facilitate communications and the exchange of commodities between the countries and in order to find an expedient solution to problems that may arise in this field.

Article 27

The construction of traffic arteries involving the territories of two or more Contracting Parties shall be achieved through joint consultations between the Parties concerned.

Article 28

The Contracting Parties shall seek to preserve and further develop the cooperation that has resulted in making their territories into one region as regards passport inspection. The inspection of passengers crossing the frontiers between the Nordic countries shall be simplified and coordinated in other respects as well. . . .

Article 30

The Contracting Parties should, whenever possible and appropriate, consult one another regarding questions of mutual interest which are dealt with by international organizations and at international conferences.

Article 31

An official in the Foreign Service of a Contracting Party who is on assignment outside the Nordic countries, shall, to the extent compatible with his official duties and if nothing gainsays it in the country to which he is appointed, also assist nationals of another Nordic country, in the event that this country has no representation in the locality concerned.

Article 32

The Contracting Parties should, whenever it is found possible and expedient, coordinate their activities for aid to and cooperation with the developing countries. . . .

Article 35[1]

In order to implement and extend Nordic cooperation under this and other agreements the Nordic countries should continuously consult with each other and when necessary coordinate measures.

Article 36[1]

Cooperation between the Nordic countries takes place within the Nordic Council, within the Nordic Council of Ministers, and at other Ministerial meetings, in special cooperation bodies and between specialist authorities.

Article 37

Provisions which have originated through cooperation between two or more of the Nordic countries may not be altered by any party unless the other parties are notified thereof. Notification is not, however, required in urgent cases or where provisions of minor importance are concerned. . .

NEW ARTICLES AGREED ON 13 FEBRUARY 1971 CONCERNING THE NORDIC COUNCIL

Article 39

The Parliaments and the Governments of the Nordic countries cooperate in the Nordic Council. The Council is an initiating and advisory body on questions concerning collaboration between these countries or some of them, and in general has those tasks which are apparent from this and other agreements.

The Faroese *Lagting* and *Landsstyre* and the Åland *Landsting* and *Landskapsstyrelse* participate in the work of the Council.

Article 40

The Council may adopt recommendations, make other representations or make statements to one or more of the Nordic countries' Governments or to the Council of Ministers.

Article 41

In addition to what may be especially agreed, the Council should be given the opportunity of stating its views on the more important

[1] Amended by the agreement of 13 February 1971.

questions of Nordic cooperation when this is not impracticable on account of shortage of time.

Article 42

The Council shall consist of seventy-eight elected members, Government representatives, and representatives of the Faroese *Landsstyre* and the Åland *Landskapsstyrelse*.

Sixteen of these members shall be elected by Denmark's *Folketing*, seventeen by Finland's *Riksdag*, six by Iceland's *Alting* and eighteen each by Norway's *Storting* and Sweden's *Riksdag*. The Faroese *Lagting* elects two members and the Åland *Landsting* one member. In addition each assembly shall elect a corresponding number of deputies.

The election of members and deputies shall take place annually and will be valid for the period up to the next election. At elections it must be ensured that different political standpoints shall be represented in the Council.

Only those persons who are members of the assembly which has performed the election may be elected members or deputy members of the Council.

Each Government shall appoint from amongst its members as many Government representatives as it wishes. The Faroese *Landsstyre* and the Åland *Landskapsstyrelse* shall each appoint one representative from amongst their members.

Article 43

Denmark's national delegation shall consist of members elected by the *Folketing* and the *Lagting* and of representatives appointed by the Government and the *Landsstyre*. Finland's delegation shall consist of members elected by the *Riksdag* and the *Landsting* and of representatives appointed by the Government and the *Landskapsstyrelse*. The delegations of the other countries shall each consist of members elected by their Parliaments and of representatives appointed by their Governments.

Article 44

The representatives of the Governments and of the *Landsstyre* and the *Landskapsstyrelse* shall have no voting rights in the Council.

On questions concerning the application of agreements between certain of the countries, only members from those countries shall be entitled to vote.

Article 45

The institutions of the Nordic Council are the Plenary Assembly, the Presidium and the Committees.

Article 46

The Plenary Assembly shall consist of all members of the Council.

The Plenary Assembly shall hold one ordinary session per annum. Extraordinary sessions may be held when the Plenary Assembly or the Presidium so decide or when at least two Governments or at least twenty-five elected members so request.

Unless otherwise decided the Council's powers shall be exercised by the Plenary Assembly.

Unless the Plenary Assembly decides otherwise, its deliberations shall be public.

Article 47

At the ordinary session the Plenary Assembly shall appoint a Presidium consisting of a president and four vice-presidents. A deputy shall be appointed for each of them. All delegations shall be represented in the Presidium and amongst the deputies. As far as possible various political standpoints shall be represented in the Presidium and amongst the deputies.

A member of the Presidium or his deputy shall be an elected member of the Council.

If an appointment as member of the Presidium or deputy thereof becomes vacant between two ordinary sessions, a new member or deputy shall be appointed for the period up to the next session by the delegation to which the member or deputy who formerly filled the appointment belonged.

The Presidium shall be responsible for handling the Council's current affairs and shall also represent the Council in general insofar as it is indicated in this agreement and in the Council's rules of procedure.

Article 48

The Plenary Assembly shall decide on the number of committees and their fields of activity. The Plenary Assembly shall also decide, in respect of each committee, how many members of each delegation are to be members of the committee. Each delegation will distribute its elected members amongst the committees accordingly.

The task of the committees is to prepare matters for consideration by the Council.

Article 49

The Council shall be assisted in its work by a Secretariat consisting of a secretary appointed by the Presidium and five secretaries, of which each delegation shall appoint one.

The Presidium shall appoint the committee secretaries and the other staff required for carrying out the Council's joint secretarial duties. Each delegation shall appoint its own Secretariat staff.

Article 50

The Governments, the Council of Ministers and the members shall have the right to submit proposals.

The proposals shall be considered in Committee before being finally dealt with by the Council.

Article 51

Recommendations shall be adopted by the Plenary Assembly on the basis of submitted proposals.

If it is not convenient to await consideration of a matter by the Plenary Assembly or if there are any other reasons for so doing, the Presidium may make other forms of representations in lieu of recommendations.

Statements are to be made by the Plenary Assembly or, in the circumstances indicated in the previous paragraph, by the Presidium.

The Presidium shall report to the Plenary Assembly on the measures taken by virtue of the second or third paragraphs of this Article.

Article 52

In the Plenary Assembly elected members may submit questions to a Government or to the Council of Ministers in respect of reports or statements furnished to the Council or in general in respect of matters concerning Nordic cooperation.

Article 53

Each country shall be responsible for defraying the expenses of its participation in the Council.

Joint expenditure shall be apportioned amongst the participating countries according to the relationship between their gross national products. In special cases, however, the Presidium may decide on some other basis of apportioning responsibility for joint costs. . . .

NEW ARTICLES AGREED ON 13 FEBRUARY 1971
CONCERNING THE NORDIC COUNCIL OF MINISTERS

Article 55

The Governments of the Nordic countries cooperate in the Nordic Council of Ministers.

The Council of Ministers shall make decisions to the extent provided for in this and other agreements between the Nordic countries. The Council of Ministers shall also be responsible for cooperation in other matters between the Governments of the Nordic countries and between the Governments and the Nordic Council.

Article 56

The Council of Ministers shall include members of each country's Government.

Each country shall appoint a Government member who, assisted by an official, shall be responsible for coordinating Nordic cooperation questions.

Article 57

The Council of ministers may make decisions only if all the Nordic countries are represented on the Council. However, in respect of questions which exclusively concern certain countries only those countries need be represented.

Each country has one vote in the Council of Ministers.

The decisions of the Council of Ministers shall be unanimous. In questions of procedure, however, decisions may be made by simple majority vote and, if the vote is indecisive, by the chairman's casting vote.

An abstention constitutes no obstacle to a decision.

Article 58

Decisions by the Council of Ministers are binding for the individual countries. However, decisions on matters which under a country's constitution require parliamentary approval are not binding until approved by parliament. If such approval is necessary the Council of Ministers shall be informed thereof before making its decision. Until parliamentary approval is given no other country is bound by the decision.

Article 59

Prior to each ordinary session of the Plenary Assembly of the Nordic
Council, the Council of Ministers shall submit a report to the Council
on Nordic cooperation. In this report the Council of Ministers shall
give a special account of the past year's cooperation and plans for
future cooperation. . . .

Article 62

Consultations between the Governments of the Nordic countries
may take place at Nordic ministerial meetings as well as in the Council
of Ministers. . . .

> Official English translation issued by the
> Nordic Council

24   Draft treaty establishing the Organization for Nordic Economic Cooperation (Nordek), 1969.

The Governments of Denmark, Finland, Norway and Sweden,

Recognizing that legal conceptions and basic ideas on economic,
social, and cultural questions coincide in the Nordic countries and are
reflected in the individual countries' public policy aims,

Having regard to the long standing cooperation between the Nordic
countries in many different spheres,

Having regard to the cooperation taking place in the Nordic
Council,

Having regard to the Nordic Agreement of 1954 on a Common
Labour Market, the Convention of 1955 on Social Security, and the
Nordic Treaty of Cooperation of 1962,

Agreeing that expanded Nordic economic cooperation will be to the
advantage both of the individual Nordic countries and of these
countries as a whole,

Assuming that the economic inter-dependence between the Nordic
countries will increase,

Being desirous of furthering economic and social development in
the Nordic countries through better utilization of the countries'
resources and a more flexible adaptation of the Nordic countries'
economic life to new and rapidly changing conditions whilst having
regard to the differences in the Nordic countries' natural conditions
and economic structures,

Being of the opinion that progress towards an extensive economic integration between the Nordic countries is facilitated by a strengthened cooperation,

Being desirous of framing economic cooperation so that it facilitates the participation of the four countries in, or their cooperation with, an enlarged European market,

Being of the opinion that Nordic cooperation should stand in conformity with the four countries' efforts to develop trade relations with third countries and to liberalize world trade, and in that context to have special regard for the interest of the developing countries,

Agreeing that Nordic economic cooperation should be carried into effect in such a way that it does not conflict with existing international commitments,

Agreeing that economic cooperation should not affect the Nordic countries' foreign and security policies,

Have therefore agreed as follows:

CHAPTER 1. INTRODUCTORY PROVISIONS

Article 1

The contracting states are agreed on extending their economic cooperation and establish through this Treaty an organization for Nordic Economic Cooperation.

Article 2

Cooperation under this Treaty aims at promoting full employment, rapid economic growth, and increased social welfare in the contracting states.

Article 3

To carry out the cooperation under this Treaty, the following institutions will be set up:

—Council of Ministers
—Permanent Committee of Government Officials
—Cooperation Committees
—Secretariat
—Consultative Committee

Article 4

Cooperation in accordance with this Treaty will take place in collaboration with the Nordic Council.

CHAPTER 2. ECONOMIC POLICY

Article 1

The contracting states regard their economic policy as a matter of common interest and they will strive to achieve the coordination of this policy and the harmonization of the instruments of economic policy which are necessary in order that Nordic economic cooperation shall operate effectively.

Article 2

The Cooperation Committee for Economic Policy will regularly discuss the economic development and the contracting states' economic policy, and will report to the Council of Ministers thereon.

These discussions shall be both on policy relating to economic trends and on long term economic policy. They will be based on existing reports and forecasts and on such additional material as the Cooperation Committee may find necessary to have prepared.

In addition the Cooperation Committee will deal with economic policy aspects of other questions arising in cooperation between the contracting states.

Article 3

The Council of Ministers shall lay down before 1 January 1974 the general lines of policy for cooperation in the field of taxation policy, budget policy, and credit policy which are necessary for implementing the provisions stated in Article 1.

Article 4

The Council of Ministers shall decide on the measures required for implementing the provisions mentioned above.

Article 5

The contracting states regard their foreign exchange policy as a question of common interest.

The contracting states should consult with each other before changing the par value of their currencies and in general on any important international foreign exchange policy question.

Article 6

A contracting state shall inform the Council of Ministers when any measures are contemplated which can appreciably affect another contracting state's economy or the economic development in the contracting states as a whole. The information should as far as possible be given in such good time that joint consultations can precede decisions on measures.

Article 7

The Council of Ministers will cause a study in regional policy to be made in order to ascertain to what extent regional policy measures may have discriminatory effects on extended economic cooperation, and to what extent the harmonization of the aims and means of that policy is appropriate.

The Council of Ministers shall lay down before 1 January 1974 the general lines of policy as regards cooperation in the field of regional policy.

CHAPTER 3. CAPITAL MOVEMENTS

Article 1

The contracting states shall gradually abolish restrictions on capital movements between the contracting states to the extent necessary to enable the Nordic market to operate effectively and in step with the progress of cooperation on economic policy in the contracting states.

The contracting states shall also as far as necessary harmonize their rules and administrative practices in respect of capital movements to and from third countries.

CHAPTER 4. TARIFF AND TRADE POLICY

Article 1

The contracting states, intending to conduct a liberal tariff and trade policy and to promote the harmonious development of world trade, and desiring to ensure the free exchange of goods between the contracting states, will set up a customs union and extend their cooperation in trade policy matters.

Article 2

1. The customs union will enter into force on 1 January 1972....

2. The common Nordic customs tariff shall have the tariff rates as stated in Annex A. . . .

Article 14

Unless otherwise provided in this Treaty quantitative import and export restrictions shall not be applied between the contracting states after 1 January 1972. . . .

CHAPTER 6. INDUSTRIAL AND ENERGY POLICY

Article 5

1. The Council of Ministers shall lay down before 1 January 1974 general principles for cooperation on the industrial and energy policy of the contracting states.

These principles shall *inter alia* indicate the fields which are specially suitable for coordinated measures or joint projects.

2. The Council of Ministers shall decide on measures for carrying out the industrial and energy policy cooperation including such decisions on the financing of projects of Nordic interest which the Council of Ministers is entitled to make under the statutes governing the General Fund.

Article 6

Through the Cooperation Committee for Industrial and Energy Policy, a contracting state shall seek consultations with other contracting states before making important decisions on industrial and energy policy matters.

CHAPTER 7. AGRICULTURAL POLICY

Article 1

1. The contracting states' agricultural policies shall be planned and implemented for the purpose of ensuring that

—the agricultural population is guaranteed a reasonable standard of living in relation to other population groups,
—that producer prices are stabilized at a reasonable level.
—that productivity in agriculture is increased through better utilization of productive resources with a view to achieving an appropriate division of labour between the states,
—that the consumers are supplied with foodstuffs at reasonable prices,

—that trade between the contracting states is expanded,
—that agricultural production is gradually adapted to the market
  potentials.

2. The contracting states shall formulate their agricultural policies
so that account is taken of

—the natural and structural differences in agricultural conditions in
  the contracting states,
—the necessity for a contracting state to maintain an agricultural
  production suited to its defence requirements. . . .

Article 3

Whilst observing their international commitments the contracting
states shall ensure that intra-Nordic trade in agricultural products
listed in Annex G which are produced in a contracting state shall take
place in such manner:

—that the contracting states are accorded an effective preference so
  that a growing proportion of the countries' import requirements
  can be covered by producers in the contracting states,
—that trade between the contracting states takes place at a
  reasonable level of prices,
—that the importing contracting state's producer price levels can be
  maintained,
—that a contracting state may be able to import from a third
  country goods to an extent which from the consumer's point of
  view is regarded as necessary. . . .

Article 5

1. The contracting states intend to cover a reasonable proportion of
their import of bread grains, feed grains and malting barley through
imports from a contracting state on condition that the products are of
satisfactory quality. . . .

Article 7

The contracting states shall set up an Agricultural Fund. The
purpose of the Fund will be to facilitate the adaptation of agriculture
to extended Nordic economic cooperation through assistance with the
financing of measures for structural changes, measures for reducing
output on non-rational farm units, and other measures intended to
help in fulfilling the aims set out in Article 1. . . .

CHAPTER 10. LABOUR MARKET AND SOCIAL POLICY

Article 1

Each contracting state will endeavour to guarantee the other contracting states' citizens who are employed in the first mentioned state the same position which their own citizens enjoy in respect of the right to work, wages, and other terms of employment.

Article 2

The contracting states shall in close cooperation expand the common Nordic Labour Market. In pursuance thereof *inter alia* common Nordic Labour Market forecasts shall be prepared and studies shall be undertaken of the extent to which the occupational and geographical mobility of labour can be increased. . . .

Expanded Nordic economic cooperation, 79–110. Report by the Nordic Committee of Government Officials. Nordisk Udrednings-serie 1969 : 17

V

Eastern Europe

The creation in January 1949 by the Soviet Union of a central agency for the coordination of the economic development of the communist countries, which took the name Council for Mutual Economic Assistance (CMEA) or Comecon (25), was only the final stage in the creation of the so-called Soviet or Eastern bloc. This had been initiated by the Russian Foreign Minister Molotov a few days after his withdrawal from the Paris Conference on 2 July 1947, a withdrawal which marked the end of any possibility of any East European country receiving Marshall Aid. In September 1947 the Communist parties of Russia, Yugoslavia, Poland, Bulgaria, Czechoslovakia, Hungary, Rumania, France and Italy met in Poland and on 5 October Molotov announced the creation of the Cominform or Communist Information Bureau. At the same time, the Molotov Plan was put into action: a system of bilateral trade agreements linking the East European countries with each other and with the Soviet Union. It was more than ten years before Comecon was given a Charter (27), and at least five years elapsed before, some time after Stalin's death in 1953, his successor Nikita Khrushchev really tried to breathe life into the new organization. It was at this time that the Comecon countries joined in a multilateral military alliance that became known as the Warsaw Pact (26). This was explicitly declared to be a counter to the re-arming of Germany and the formation of Western European Union (6). It certainly was used by the Soviet Union to extend and consolidate her military and political presence in Europe in much the same way as NATO has the effect of extending American power. In each case the decisive nuclear arm was kept firmly in the control of the main partner in the alliance.

The Communist Bloc in Eastern Europe has always been beset by inner struggles, partly because of the very disparate economies of its Member States. Stalin and Tito quarrelled in 1948, the very year when the bloc was put together; there was a revolt in the German

Democratic Republic in 1953; and troubles in Poland and Hungary in
1956. Later it was the Albanians who resented or defied Moscow. The
criticism of the Common Market published by the Russian Institute of
World Economics, which forms part of the Department of Economics
of the Soviet Academy of Sciences, in 1957 (31), was probably
subscribed to gladly in all Eastern bloc countries. But this was by no
means true of the 'international socialist division of labour', as
expounded at the end of 1961 (28). This Khrushchevian elaboration of
the theory of the integration of complementary economies to form a
rational whole, fell foul of the Rumanians in particular. To put it in an
extreme form, was it fair that the already heaviiy industrialized
economies of the German Democratic Republic and Czechoslovakia
should be still further expanded, while the Bulgarians and Rumanians
remained content with growing vegetables, as it were, for the rest of
the bloc? No wonder the Rumanian Communist Party's Central
Committee came out strongly in April 1964 against integration
and, in particular, against any supranational planning authority
(29). Partly because of differences in their economies and their
political attitudes, the Eastern bloc countries have shown no sign
of becoming significantly more unified in the last decade, even though
the doings of Comecon regularly provide material for the official
weekly *Soviet News*.

25 Communiqué announcing the establishment of the Council for Mutual Economic Assistance (Comecon), January 1949

An economic conference of representatives of Bulgaria, Hungary,
Poland, Rumania, the USSR and Czechoslovakia was held this month
in Moscow.

The conference noted the fact of considerable success in the
development of economic relations among the above-mentioned
countries, which found expression, first and foremost, in a major
increase of trade exchange.

Due to the establishment of the above-mentioned economic
relations and to the implementation of the policy of economic
cooperation, the [countries of] people's democracy and the USSR had
the opportunity of speeding up the restoration and development of
their respective national economies.

The conference established further that the Governments of the
United States of America, Britain, and of certain other countries of
Western Europe, had been, as a matter of fact, boycotting trade

relations with the countries of people's democracy and with the USSR, since these countries did not consider it possible to submit to the Marshall Plan dictate, as this plan violated the sovereignty of the countries and the interests of their national economies.

In view of the above-mentioned circumstances, the conference discussed the possibility of organizing broader economic cooperation among the countries of people's democracy and the USSR.

The conference decided that in order to establish still broader economic cooperation among the countries of people's democracy and the USSR it was necessary to institute a Council for Economic Mutual Assistance, comprising representatives of the countries taking part in the conference, on the basis of equal representation, and having as its task the exchange of experience in the economic field, the rendering of technical assistance to one another and the rendering of mutual assistance in regard to raw materials, foodstuffs, machinery, equipment, etc.

The conference stated that the Council for Economic Mutual Assistance shall be an open organization, which may be joined by other countries of Europe that share the principles of the Council for Economic Mutual Assistance and the desire to participate in broad economic cooperation with the above-mentioned countries.

The Council for Economic Mutual Assistance shall pass decisions only with the consent of the country concerned.

The Council shall meet periodically, in the capitals of the signatory countries in turn, under the chairmanship of the representative of that country in whose capital the session takes place.

Soviet News, 25 January 1949

26 Treaty of Friendship, Cooperation and Mutual Assistance, signed at Warsaw, 14 May 1955

The contracting parties,

Reaffirming their desire for the organization of a system of collective security in Europe, with the participation of all the European states, irrespective of their social and state systems, which would make it possible to combine their efforts in the interests of securing peace in Europe,

Taking into consideration at the same time the situation obtaining in Europe as the result of ratification of the Paris agreements, which provide for the formation of a new military grouping in the shape of the 'Western European Union' together with a remilitarized Western

Germany, and for the integration of Western Germany in the North Atlantic bloc, which increases the threat of another war and creates a menace to the national security of the peaceloving states,

Convinced that, under these circumstances, the peaceloving states of Europe should take the necessary measures for safeguarding their security, and in the interests of maintaining peace in Europe,

Guided by the purposes and principles of the United Nations Charter,

In the interests of further strengthening and promoting friendship, cooperation and mutual assistance, in accordance with the principles of respect for the independence and sovereignty of states, and also with the principle of non-interference in their internal affairs,

Have resolved to conclude this Treaty of Friendship, Cooperation and Mutual Assistance, and have appointed as their authorized representatives:

[The names of the plenipotentiaries of Albania, Bulgaria, Hungary, East Germany, Poland, Rumania, the Soviet Union and Czechoslovakia follow].

Article 1

The contracting parties undertake, in accordance with the Charter of the United Nations Organization, to refrain in their international relations from the threat or use of force, and to settle their international disputes by peaceful means so as not to endanger international peace and security.

Article 2

The contracting parties declare their readiness to take part, in the spirit of sincere cooperation, in all international undertakings intended to safeguard international peace and security and they shall use all their energies for the realization of these aims.

Moreover, the contracting parties shall work for the adoption, in agreement with other states desiring to cooperate in this matter, of effective measures towards a general reduction of armaments and prohibition of atomic, hydrogen and other weapons of mass destruction.

Article 3

The contracting parties shall take council among themselves on all important international questions relating to their common interests, guided by the interests of strengthening international peace and security.

They shall take council among themselves immediately, whenever, in the opinion of any of them, there has arisen the threat of an armed attack on one or several states that are signatories of the treaty, in the interests of organizing their joint defence and of upholding peace and security.

Article 4

In the event of an armed attack in Europe on one or several states that are signatories of the treaty by any state or group of states, each state that is a party to this treaty shall, in the exercise of the right to individual or collective self-defence in accordance with Article 51 of the Charter of the United Nations Organization, render the state or states so attacked immediate assistance, individually and in agreement with other states that are parties to this treaty, by all the means it may consider necessary, including the use of armed force. The states that are parties to this treaty shall immediately take council among themselves concerning the necessary joint measures to be adopted for the purpose of restoring and upholding international peace and security.

In accordance with the principles of the Charter of the United Nations Organization, the Security Council shall be advised of the measures taken on the basis of the present article. These measures shall be stopped as soon as the Security Council has taken the necessary measures for restoring and upholding international peace and security.

Article 5

The contracting parties have agreed on the establishment of a joint command for their armed forces, which shall be placed, by agreement among these parties, under this command, which shall function on the basis of jointly defined principles. They shall also take other concerted measures necessary for strengthening their defence capacity, in order to safeguard the peaceful labour of their peoples, to guarantee the inviolability of their frontiers and territories and to provide safeguards against possible aggression.

Article 6

For the purpose of holding the consultations provided for in the present treaty among the states that are parties to the treaty, and for the purpose of considering problems arising in connection with the implementation of this treaty, a Political Consultative Committee shall be formed in which each state that is a party to this treaty shall be represented by a member of the government, or any other specially appointed representative.

The committee may form the auxiliary organs for which the need may arise.

Article 7

The contracting parties undertake not to participate in any coalitions and alliances, and not to conclude any agreements the purposes of which would be at variance with those of the present treaty.

The contracting parties declare that their obligations under existing international treaties are not at variance with the provisions of this treaty.

Article 8

The contracting parties declare that they will act in the spirit of friendship and cooperation with the object of furthering the development of, and strengthening the economic and cultural relations between them [sic], adhering to the principles of mutual respect for their independence and sovereignty, and of non-interference in their internal affairs.

Article 9

The present treaty is open to be acceded to by other states—irrespective of their social and state systems—which may express their readiness to assist, through participation in the present treaty, in combining the efforts of the peaceloving states for the purpose of safeguarding the peace and security of nations. This act of acceding to the treaty shall become effective, with the consent of the states that are parties to this treaty, after the instrument of accedence has been deposited with the government of the Polish People's Republic.

Article 10

The present treaty is subject to ratification, and the instruments of ratification shall be deposited with the government of the Polish People's Republic.

The treaty shall take effect on the date on which the last ratification instrument is deposited. The government of the Polish People's Republic shall advise the other states that are parties to the treaty of each ratification instrument deposited with it.

Article 11

The present treaty shall remain in force for twenty years. For the contracting parties which will not have submitted to the government of the Polish People's Republic a statement denouncing the treaty a year before the expiration of its term, it shall remain in force throughout the following ten years.

In the event of the organization of a system of collective security in Europe and the conclusion of a general European treaty of collective security to that end, which the contracting parties shall unceasingly seek to bring about, the present treaty shall cease to be effective on the date the general European treaty comes into force.

Done in Warsaw, on 14 May 1955, in one copy each in the Russian, Polish, Czech, and German languages, all the texts being equally authentic. Certified copies of the present treaty shall be transmitted by the government of the Polish People's Republic to all the parties to this treaty.

In witness whereof the authorized representatives have signed the present treaty and have affixed thereto their seals

Communiqué setting up a Joint Command of the armed forces of the signatories to the Treaty of Warsaw, 14 May 1955

Under the Treaty of Friendship, Cooperation and Mutual Assistance between the People's Republic of Albania, the People's Republic of Bulgaria, the Hungarian People's Republic, the German Democratic Republic, the Polish People's Republic, the Rumanian People's Republic, the Union of Soviet Socialist Republics and the Czecho-slovak Republic, the states that are parties to the treaty have taken the decision to form a joint command of their armed forces.

This decision envisages that general questions pertaining to the strengthening of the defence capacity and to the organization of the joint armed forces of the states that are parties to the treaty will be examined by the Political Consultative Committee, which will take appropriate decisions.

I. S. Koniev, Marshal of the Soviet Union, has been appointed commander-in-chief of the joint armed forces allotted by the states that are signatories to the treaty.

The assistants appointed for the commander-in-chief of the joint armed forces are the Ministers of Defence and other military leaders of the states that are parties to the treaty, who are vested with the command of the armed forces of each state that is a party to the treaty, allotted to the joint armed forces.

The question of participation of the German Democratic Republic in measures pertaining to the armed forces of the joint command will be examined later.

A staff of the joint armed forces of the states that are parties to the treaty will be set up under the commander-in-chief of the joint armed forces and this staff will include permanent representatives of the general staffs of the states that are parties to the treaty.

The headquarters of the staff will be in Moscow.

Distribution of the joint armed forces on the territories of states that are parties to the treaty will be carried out in accordance with the requirements of mutual defence in agreement among these states.

Soviet News, 16 May 1955

27 Charter of the Council for Mutual Economic Assistance (Comecon) approved at Sofia, 14 December 1959, as amended by the Sixteenth and Seventeenth Sessions of the Council

The Governments of the People's Republic of Albania, the People's Republic of Bulgaria, the Czechoslovak Republic, the German Democratic Republic, the Hungarian People's Republic, the Polish People's Republic, the Rumanian People's Republic and the Union of Soviet Socialist Republics,

Taking into account that economic cooperation, successfully effected between their countries, contributes to the most rational development of the national economy, the elevation of the living standards of the population, and the strengthening of the unity and cohesion of these countries,

Fully resolved to continue developing all-round economic cooperation on the basis of the consistent implementation of the international socialist division of labour in the interests of building socialism and communism in their countries and ensuring a lasting peace throughout the world,

Convinced that the development of economic cooperation between their countries promotes the achievement of the purposes expounded in the Charter of the United Nations,

Confirming their readiness to develop economic relations with all countries, irrespective of their social and state systems, on the principles of equality, mutual advantage, and non-interference in domestic affairs.

Recognizing the ever growing role of the Council for Mutual Economic Assistance in organizing economic cooperation between their countries,

Have agreed for these purposes to adopt the present Charter.

Article 1 : Purposes and Principles

1. The purpose of the Council for Mutual Economic Assistance is to facilitate, by uniting and coordinating the efforts of the Council's member countries, the planned development of the national economy, acceleration of economic and technical progress in these countries, a rise in the level of industrialization in countries with less developed industries, uninterrupted growth of labour productivity and a steady advance of the welfare of the peoples in the Council's member countries.

2. The Council for Mutual Economic Assistance is based on the principles of the sovereign equality of all member countries of the Council.

The economic, scientific and technical cooperation of the Council's member countries shall be effected in conformity with the principles of full equality, respect for sovereignty and national interests, mutual advantage, and comradely mutual assistance.

Article 2 : Membership

1. The founder members of the Council for Mutual Economic Assistance shall be the countries which sign and ratify the present Charter.

2. Membership in the Council is open to other countries which subscribe to the purposes and principles of the Council and agree to assume obligations contained in the present Charter.

The admission of new members shall be effected by decision of the Session of the Council on the basis of official applications by countries for membership in the Council.

3. Each member country of the Council may withdraw from the Council by notice to that effect given to the depositary of the present Charter. Such notice shall come into force six months after its receipt

by the depositary. Upon receipt of such notice the depositary shall accordingly inform the member countries of the Council.

4. The member countries of the Council agree:

(a) to ensure the fulfilment of the recommendations of the Council organs adopted by them;

(b) to render the Council and its officials the necessary cooperation in the discharge of their functions under the present Charter;

(c) to submit to the Council materials and information necessary for carrying out the tasks assigned to it;

(d) to inform the Council about progress in fulfilling the recommendations adopted in the Council.

Article 3: Functions and Powers

1. In conformity with the purposes and principles mentioned in Article 1 of the present Charter, the Council for Mutual Economic Assistance shall:

(a) organize all-round economic, scientific and technical cooperation of the Council's member countries in the most rational use of their natural resources and acceleration of the development of their productive forces;

(b) foster the improvement of the international socialist division of labour by coordinating national economic development plans, and the specialization and cooperation of production in the Council's member countries;

(c) take measures to study economic, scientific and technical problems which are of interest to the Council's member countries;

(d) assist the Council's member countries in elaborating and carrying out joint measures for:

the development of the industry and agriculture of the Council's member countries;

the development of transport with a view to ensuring first priority for increasing export, import and transit shipments of the Council's member countries;

the most efficient use of principal capital investments allocated by the Council's member countries for the development of the mining and manufacturing industries and for the construction of major projects which are of interest to two countries or more;

the development of trade and exchange of services between the Council's member countries and between them and other countries;

the exchange of scientific and technical achievements and advanced production experience;

   (e) take such other actions as may be required for the achievement of the purposes of the Council.

   2. The Council for Mutual Economic Assistance, as represented by its organs, acting within the terms of their reference, is authorized to adopt recommendations and decisions in accordance with the present Charter.

Article 4: Recommendations and Decisions

   1. Recommendations shall be made on questions of economic, scientific and technical cooperation. Recommendations shall be submitted for consideration to the Council's member countries.

   Recommendations adopted by the Council's member countries shall be implemented by decision of the Governments or competent organs of these countries in conformity with their laws.

   2. Decisions shall be adopted on organizational and procedural matters. Decisions shall enter into force, unless otherwise stipulated in the decisions themselves, as of the day the meeting's protocol is signed by the appropriate organ of the Council.

   3. All recommendations and decisions of the Council shall be adopted only with the consent of the interested member countries of the Council, each country having the right to declare its interest in any question considered by the Council.

   Recommendations and decisions shall not apply to countries which declare that they have no interest in the given question. Each of these countries, however, may subsequently join recommendations or decisions adopted by the rest of the Council's member countries.

Article 5: Organs

   1. To exercise the functions and powers under Article 3 of the present Charter, the Council for Mutual Economic Assistance shall have the following principal organs:

Session of the Council
Executive Committee
Standing Commissions
Secretariat.

   2. Such other organs as may be found necessary shall be established in accordance with the present Charter.

Article 6: Session of the Council

1. The Session of the Council shall be the highest organ of the Council for Mutual Economic Assistance. It may discuss all questions within the terms of reference of the Council and adopt recommendations and decisions in accordance with the present Charter.

2. The Session of the Council shall consist of delegations of all the Council's member countries. The composition of the delegation of each country shall be determined by the Government of the country concerned.

3. Regular Sessions of the Council shall be convened at least once a year on a rotational basis in the capitals of the member countries of the Council under the chairmanship of the head of the delegation of the host country.

4. An emergency Session of the Council may be convened at the request or with the consent of not less than one-third of the Council's member countries.

5. The Session of the Council shall:

(a) consider:
fundamental questions of economic, scientific and technical cooperation and determine major policies of the Council;
the report of the Executive Committee on the activities of the Council;

    (b) exercise such other functions as may be found necessary for the achievement of the purposes of the Council.

6. The Session of the Council may establish such organs as it deems necessary for the discharge of the Council's functions.

7. The Session of the Council shall adopt its own rules of procedure.

Article 7: Executive Committee of the Council

1. The Executive Committee of the Council for Mutual Economic Assistance shall consist of representatives of all the member countries of the Council, one from each country, at a level of the Deputy Head of the Government.

The Executive Committee shall be the principal executive organ of the Council.

The Executive Committee shall have a Bureau for consolidated problems of economic plans on which every member country of the

Council shall be represented by the deputy chairman of the state planning body.

2. The Executive Committee shall hold its meetings at least once every two months.

3. The Executive Committee, within its terms of reference, shall be entitled to adopt recommendations and decisions in accordance with this Charter. The Executive Committee may submit proposals for consideration by the Session of the Council. . . .

Article 8 : Standing Commissions

1. The Standing Commissions of the Council for Mutual Economic Assistance shall be established by the Session of the Council for the purpose of promoting the further development of economic ties between the Council's member countries and the organization of multilateral economic, scientific and technical cooperation in individual branches of the national economy of these countries.

Regulations governing the Standing Commissions shall be approved by the Executive Committee of the Council.

2. Each member country of the Council shall appoint its representatives to the Standing Commissions. . . .

4. . . . The Standing Commissions shall submit annual reports on the work done and their future activity to the Executive Committee of the Council.

5. Meetings of the Standing Commissions shall be held, as a rule, in their regular seats which shall be determined by the Session of the Council. . . .

Article 9 : Secretariat

1. The Secretariat of the Council for Mutual Economic Assistance shall comprise a Secretary of the Council, his deputies and such staff as may be required for the discharge of the Secretariat's functions.

The Secretary of the Council shall be appointed by the Session of the Council and his deputies by the Executive Committee of the Council. The Secretary of the Council and his deputies shall direct the work of the Secretariat of the Council. The staff of the Secretariat shall be recruited from among citizens of the Council's member countries under the Regulations governing the Secretariat of the Council.

The Secretary of the Council shall be the chief official of the Council. He shall represent the Council in relations with officials and organizations of the Council's member countries, other countries and international organizations. The Secretary of the Council may empower his deputies and also Secretariat officials to act on his behalf. . . .

4. The seat of the Secretariat shall be in Moscow.

Article 11: Relations with International Organizations

The Council for Mutual Economic Assistance may establish and maintain relations with economic organizations of the United Nations and other international organizations.

The character and form of such relations shall be determined by the Council in agreement with the relevant international organizations.

Article 14: Languages

The languages of all the member countries of the Council shall be the official languages of the Council for Mutual Economic Assistance.

The Russian language shall be the working language of the Council.

> English translation supplied by the Comecon Secretariat, Moscow

28 Basic principles of international socialist division of labour, approved by the Comecon Council in Warsaw, 12–15 December 1961

1. Community of socialist countries and international socialist division of labour. The world socialist system is a social, economic and political community of free, sovereign nations following the path of socialism and communism, united by common interests and goals and by indestructible ties of international socialist solidarity.

The close union of the socialist countries within a single system is necessitated by the objective laws of economic and political development. . . .

The community of socialist countries achieves its aims through all-round political, economic and cultural cooperation, with all the socialist countries guided by the principles of full equality, mutual respect for each other's independence and sovereignty, fraternal assistance and mutual benefit. No member of the socialist camp has, or can have, any special rights or privileges. Adherence to the principles of Marxism–Leninism and socialist internationalism is an indispensable condition for the successful development of the world socialist system. . . .

Each socialist country maps out its own economic development plans based on the concrete conditions in the given country, the

political and economic goals·set by the Communist and Workers'
Parties, and the needs and potentialities of all the socialist countries.
The new social system makes it possible organically to combine the
development of each national economy with the development and
consolidation of the world economic system of socialism as a whole.
The progress of the entire world socialist system depends on the
contribution of each country.

The socialist countries consider it their internationalist duty to
direct their efforts to securing a high rate of development in the
industry and agriculture of each country commensurate with available
potentialities, progressively equalizing economic development levels,
and successfully solving the problem of exceeding the world capitalist
system in absolute volume of industrial and agricultural production
and subsequently surpassing the economically most developed
capitalist countries in per capita production and in living standards of
the working people. . . .

In contrast to international capitalist division of labour, which
reflects the exploitation of the weak by the strong and is formed
spontaneously, through sharp monopoly rivalry and expansion,
accentuating unequal economic development levels and producing an
ugly, one-sided economic structure in underdeveloped countries,
international socialist division of labour is carried out consciously,
according to plan, in conformity with the vital interests of the peoples
and with the aim of ensuring harmonious and all-round development
of all the socialist countries, and adding strength to their unity.

Planned international socialist division of labour makes for
maximum utilization of the advantages of the world socialist system,
for a balanced economy in each country, rational distribution of the
productive forces throughout the world socialist system, efficient
employment of labour and material resources, and enhancement of
the defence potential of the socialist camp. Division of labour must
guarantee each country the possibility to market its specialized
products and to buy the necessary raw materials, equipment and other
goods.

The objectives of international socialist division of labour are more
efficient social production, a higher rate of economic growth, higher
living standards for the working people in all the socialist countries,
industrialization and gradual removal of historical differences in
the economic development levels of the socialist countries, and the
creation of a material basis for their more-or-less simultaneous
transition to communism, within one and the same historical era.

At the same time, international socialist division of labour helps to accomplish the basic tasks facing each socialist country and the whole of the world socialist system at each historical stage.

International socialist division of labour takes into account the world division of labour. By expanding their economic ties with all countries of the world, the socialist countries thus strengthen the material basis for peaceful co-existence of the two world socio-economic systems. . . .

2. *Co-ordination of economic plans—the principal means of successfully developing and extending international socialist division of labour.* . . . CMEA experience in economic cooperation has shown that coordination of plans should seek to implement the following inter-related objective principles of international socialist division of labour:

—adequate assessment of the objectively required proportions in the economic development of each country and the world socialist system as a whole, so as to attain a balanced economy in each country;
—high economic efficiency of international socialist division of labour, i.e. a high rate of growth in production and maximum satisfaction of the needs of the population in each country with minimum expenditure of social labour;
—combination of international specialization in production with all-round, comprehensive development of the economies of the individual socialist countries with a view to the fullest and most rational utilization in all the countries of natural and economic resources, including manpower;
—steady elimination of historic differences in the economic development levels of the individual countries, primarily through industrialization of countries with relatively low economic levels, and through maximum utilization of the internal potentialities of each country and of the advantages inherent in the world socialist system. . . .

The interconnection between the economies of the individual countries, stemming from division of labour, should be strong and stable, for any deviation, even by a single country, would inevitably lead to disturbances in the economic cycle in the other socialist countries.

Coordination of economic plans should take the fullest account of the necessity to produce, within the framework of the world socialist system, staple goods in quantities sufficient to meet the needs of the socialist countries with due allowances for their ever-expanding trade with other countries. . . .

3. Basic directions in rational division of labour in key branches of the economy. . . . Interstate specialization implies concentrating production of similar products in one or several socialist countries so as to meet the needs of all interested countries, thus improving industrial techniques and management, and establishing stable economic ties and cooperation. International specialization should serve to expand production, reduce costs, raise productivity and improve quality and technical standards.

As a stimulating factor of technical progress, international specialization and cooperation in production help the rapid industrialization of all the socialist countries.

International specialization and cooperation are potent economic factors in the development of all industries, especially engineering, chemicals, ferrous and nonferrous metallurgy. Specialization permits a rapid change-over to new types of goods, the manufacture of which is made possible by technical progress. . . .

Every encouragement [must] be given to the production in all the countries of the materials scarce in the socialist camp, taking into account natural and economic conditions. . . .

6. Elimination of historic differences in economic development levels of the socialist countries. When they set out to build a socialist society, the countries of the world socialist system differed in level of development of their productive forces. The very nature of socialism dictates equalization of these levels. . . .

In the course of building socialism and communism there will be eliminated the substantial differences in the level of development of national productive forces, differences that stem from the historic conditions of capitalist development. . . .

To enhance the effect of these countries' efforts in accelerated economic expansion, the other socialist countries:

—share their advanced knowledge in science and technology;
—help in designing modern plants, prospecting and exploration, and in the training of skilled personnel;
—supply industrial equipment, notably complete plant, and assist with its installation and adjustment;
—grant credits and other forms of aid. . . .

7. Division of labour and trade between socialist countries. International socialist division of labour is the basis for trade between the socialist countries, which is carried out on the principle of equivalent exchange. . . .

Multilateral coordination of plans and the resultant recommendations for specialization and cooperation should ensure that each socialist country has a balanced payments structure, notably through wider use of multilateral settlements. . . .

It is necessary continually to perfect the system of price formation on the world socialist market in keeping with the requirements of the planned extension of the international socialist division of labour, steady expansion of trade, and accelerated development of the world socialist economy, while creating conditions for the gradual change-over to an independent price basis. . . .

As economic cooperation between the socialist countries grows in strength and scope and more experience is gained in international specialization and cooperation of production, the principles of international socialist division of labour formulated here will be perfected, elaborated and enlarged.

> M. Kaser, *Comecon. Integration problems of the planned economies*, 249–54. Second edition, Oxford, 1967

29   Declaration of the Enlarged Plenum of the Central Committee of the Rumanian Workers' Party held from 15 to 22 April 1964

. . . The successes obtained by the Rumanian People's Republic and by the other socialist countries show that the successful solution of the tasks of developing the economy depends first and foremost on the utilization of each country's internal possibilities, through an intense mustering of its own forces and the maximum use of its natural resources. Decisive for the development of the countries that inherited economic backwardness from capitalism is socialist industrialization, the only road that ensures the harmonious, balanced, and ever ascending as well as rapid growth of the whole national economy, the continuous rise of the productivity of social labour, the intensive and complex development of agriculture, the systematic improvement in the people's living standards. The results obtained by our country in all fields of socialist construction are indissolubly linked to this policy, which is consistently pursued by the Rumanian Workers' Party.

At the same time the economic and technical-scientific progress of the socialist countries relies on the relations of cooperation and mutual assistance established among them. These fruitful relations have seen a steady development; they have proved their efficiency, making a particularly important contribution to the successes scored by the socialist countries.

With a view to the complete utilization of the advantages of these relations, the Council for Mutual Economic Aid was set up. According to its statutes it aims to contribute, through the uniting and coordination of efforts, to the development of the national economy, to speeding up economic and technological progress, to raising the level of industrialization of the less developed countries, to the steady increase in labour productivity, and to the ceaseless improvement in the welfare of the peoples in the member countries.

Cooperation within CMEA is achieved on the basis of the principles of fully equal rights, of observance of national sovereignty and interests, of mutual advantage and comradely assistance.

As concerns the method of economic cooperation, the socialist countries that are members of CMEA have established that the main means of achieving the international socialist division of labour, the main form of cooperation among their national economies, is to coordinate plans on the basis of bilateral and multilateral agreements.

During the development of the relations of cooperation among the socialist countries that are members of CMEA, forms and measures have been projected, such as a joint plan and a single planning body for all member countries, interstate technical-productive branch unions, enterprises jointly owned by several countries, interstate economic complexes, etc.

Our party has very clearly expressed its point of view, declaring that, since the essence of the projected measures lies in shifting some functions of economic management from the competence of the respective state to that of superstate bodies or organisms, these measures are not in keeping with the principles that underlie the relations among the socialist countries.

The idea of a single planning body for all CMEA countries has the most serious economic and political implications. The planned management of the national economy is one of the fundamental, essential, and inalienable attributes of the sovereignty of the socialist state—the state plan being the chief means through which the socialist state achieves its political and socioeconomic objectives, establishes the directions and rates of development of the national economy, its fundamental proportions, the accumulations, the measures for raising the people's living standard and cultural level. The sovereignty of the socialist state requires that it effectively and fully avail itself of the means for the practical implementation of these functions, holding in its hands all the levers of managing economic and social life. Transmitting such levers to the competence of superstate or extrastate bodies would turn sovereignty into a meaningless notion.

All these are also fully valid as concerns interstate technical-productive branch unions as well as enterprises commonly owned by two or several states. The state plan is one and indivisible; no parts or sections can be separated from it in order to be transferred outside the state. The management of the national economy as a whole is not possible if the questions of managing some branches or enterprises are taken away from the competence of the party and government of the respective country and transferred to extrastate bodies. . . .

> *Sino-Soviet relations, 1964–1965*, ed. W. E.
> Griffith, 282–3. The M.I.T. Press,
> Cambridge, Mass.

VI
Ideas and pressure groups,
1956–1963

One of the most influential pro-European pressure groups was the Action Committee for the United States of Europe, a purely private committee set up by Jean Monnet in 1955 after he had resigned from his Presidency of the High Authority of the ECSC. It has been somewhat unkindly said that the annual meeting of the Committee was in reality just Monnet and his friends; and that during the rest of the time the Committee was Monnet himself, with a small secretariat. In fact the Committee brought together all political parties, except the Gaullists and the communists and a number of leading trade unions from different countries; and its annual declarations, the text of the first of which follows (30), made some impression on public opinion. In many cases indeed, Monnet directly helped to determine government policy. Apart from the *Seventeen Theses*, the remaining documents in this chapter date from 1962–3; they illustrate the attitudes of politicians and intellectuals in various countries to European integration and the Common Market. De Gaulle's press conference of 15 May 1962 (32) is one among many, but it may be considered typical—typically voluble, lively and in a certain way nationalist; by no means 'European'. The Russian view of the Common Market as a capitalist, neo-colonialist conspiracy was expounded at length in the *Seventeen Theses* (31) of 1957, already mentioned, as well as, more pithily, in May 1962, by the leading statesman of the country—N. Khrushchev (33). On the other hand a year later President Kennedy expressed continuing American sympathy and encouragement for European integration (35).

The programme embodied in the European Movement's Memorandum of June 1962 (34), of further integration of a political character within the framework of the Common Market, has still for the most part not been implemented. Yet it has been professed ever since by many of Europe's leading statesmen. The document is thus notable for the way it points to the lack of progress during the remainder of the 1960s and into the 1970s: it is indeed a commentary on Chapter 7 as a whole. There is a tongue-in-cheek element in the declaration of the European socialists printed at the end of this section (36). Surely 'Europe' has been created by the right, not the left, wing parties? But the criticism of the Franco-German Treaty expressed here has more to do with European integration than the Treaty itself, which has been omitted.

30   Resolution and Joint Declaration of the Action Committee for the United States of Europe, 18 January 1956

Resolution setting forth the reasons for the Joint Declaration

1. Our organizations, political parties and trade unions, joining together for the first time over and above the national issues that may divide them, are unanimous in the belief that the hopes of our peoples for improvements in living conditions, for justice, freedom, and peace will not be fulfilled if each nation tries to work alone. Our countries must pool their energies and resources. That is why we have taken the initiative in forming the Action Committee for the United States of Europe. The Committee will bring about unity of action among its member organizations in order to attain by successive concrete achievements the United States of Europe.

The Committee stresses that it remains open to all similar organizations in other European countries which declare themselves to be in agreement with the avowed principles and the objectives pursued by it. It refuses to consider as final the present situation in which the organizations of only six European countries have been able to give their agreement, and unanimously renews its hope of seeing other European countries taking without reservations the place that is theirs in the building of Europe, or at the very least associating themselves closely in that effort.

2. The action of the Committee and of the participating organizations will consist first of all in making clear to Governments, Parliaments, and public opinion that the Committeee and its constituent organizations are determined that the Resolution agreed on at Messina on 2 June last by the Foreign Ministers of Belgium, France, Germany, Italy, Luxembourg, and the Netherlands, becomes a real step towards the United States of Europe.

Just as the six Foreign Ministers declared in their Resolution at Messina on 1–2 June 1955, so too do our organizations believe that the establishment of a united Europe must be pursued by the development of common institutions, the progressive merger of national economies, the creation of a common market, and the progressive harmonization of social policies.

In Brussels, experts of the 'Intergovernmental Committee created by the Messina Conference' have studied the technical problems posed by that Resolution. They have submitted their reports. In the near future the Governments will have to make the necessary decisions to translate the experts' conclusions into actual achievements.

Among these achievements that our Committee wants to be realized, the one that could and should be most rapidly carried out concerns atomic energy.

3. The development of atomic energy for peaceful uses opens the prospect of a new industrial revolution and the possibility of a profound change in living and working conditions.

Together, our countries are capable of themselves developing a nuclear industry. They form the only region in the world that can attain the same level as the great world Powers. Yet separately they will not be able to overcome their time-lag which is a consequence of European disunity.

Action is urgently needed if Europe is not to let her opportunity pass by.

An atomic industry producing atomic energy will inevitably be able to produce bombs. For that reason the political aspects and the economic aspects of atomic energy are inseparable. The European Community must develop atomic energy exclusively for peaceful purposes. This choice requires a water-tight system of control. It opens the way to general control on a world-wide scale. It in no way affects the implementation of international agreements already in force.

Mere cooperation among Governments will not suffice to achieve these objectives. It is indispensable that our States delegate the necessary powers and give the necessary common mandate to European institutions.

4. In order that the necessary measures may be taken rapidly, we have agreed to submit the attached declaration for Parliamentary approval in Belgium, France, Germany, Italy, Luxembourg, and the Netherlands, and to invite our Governments to conclude without delay a Treaty conforming to the rules set forth therein.

'5. Lastly, the Committee has decided to meet again on 5 April 1956 to examine the following points:

Parliamentary approval of the attached joint declaration concerning atomic energy;
decisions to be taken on the necessary measures for supporting the actions of the Governments for implementation of the Messina Resolution, particularly as regards the progressive establishment of the Common Market.

Joint declaration to be submitted for Parliamentary approval in Belgium, France, Germany, Italy, Luxembourg, and the Netherlands, adopted unanimously on 18 January 1956.

1. In order to bring about an exclusively peaceful development of atomic energy, as well as to ensure the security of workers and populations and to improve the standard of living of the populations;
In order to facilitate the work and progress of the industries concerned:

by ensuring a sufficient supply of nuclear fuels;
by financial and technical assistance;
by the creation of essential common services and establishments;
by the creation of a common market for special materials and equipment defined by the Commission; and
by the pooling of knowledge;

it is indispensable that our countries jointly delegate to a European Commission for Atomic Energy the necessary powers and the necessary common mandate.

2. In order to guarantee the exclusively peaceful character of nuclear activities as well as to guarantee the security of labour forces and populations, the Commission should establish a system of control. It is indispensable:

(a) On the one hand, that exclusively for that purpose, all nuclear fuels produced in, or imported into, the territories coming under the jurisdiction of our countries be acquired by the European Commission for Atomic Energy. This rule shall not affect the carrying out of international agreements already in force. The Commission must retain exclusive ownership of nuclear fuels throughout their processing. The Commission will place such fuels at the disposal of users equitably and without discrimination, in periods of normal supply as well as in time of shortage.

(b) On the other hand, that the construction and operation of nuclear installations be subject to prior authorization by the Commission, to be issued when the conditions are fulfilled allowing the Commission to follow the processing and use of such fuels and to maintain the security of workers and populations.

Security rules to be observed in the transportation and handling of nuclear materials, the construction and operation of installations, and the disposal of waste should be laid down by the Commission in cooperation with international organizations, particularly the UN. The Commission will ensure the application of these rules.

3. Parliamentary control over the Commission should be exercised by the Common Assembly and juridical control by the Court of Justice of the ECSC.

The number of members of the Common Assembly should be increased in view of its new tasks.

The Special Council of Ministers should harmonize the activities of the Commission with those of the national Governments responsible for the general economic policy of their countries.

A Consultative Committee composed of workers, employers, and consumers should be attached to the Commission.

4. Every opportunity for participation in the Community must be open to European countries other than our own.

(a) These European countries must be able to participate fully if they accept the above rules. The more numerous the participating countries, the more profitable the common effort will be to each.

(b) In particular, everything must be done to obtain the full participation of Great Britain. If Great Britain does not accept full participation, the necessary measures should in any case be taken to ensure her close association.

(c) Finally, possibilities should be open to European non-member countries for using the common services and establishments, or for participating in their setting-up, in accordance with special agreements to be concluded later.

The Commission alone should be empowered to negotiate and conclude all agreements with third countries necessary for the accomplishment of its mission, particularly in matters concerning the supply of nuclear materials.

The rights and obligations of the participating countries resulting from agreements in force relative to the peaceful uses of atomic energy should be transferred to the Commission, subject to the consent of the third countries with which these agreements have been concluded.

Action Committee for the United States of Europe:
statements and declarations, 1955–1967, 12–16
London, Chatham House, 1969

31 The *Seventeen Theses* on the Common Market, issued by the Institute of World Economics and International Relations, Moscow, 1957

1. . . . The agreements on the Common Market, Euratom and Eurafrica have a history. They form the continuation of a whole series of initatives designed to promote the so-called 'integration' of Europe. The Western powers have pursued this integration in various directions throughout the entire post-war period: economic, political, ideological and above all military. In the economic sphere they have had recourse, for this purpose, to measues like the creation of Benelux, the OEEC and the European Payments Union, and the ECSC. To promote political and ideological integration they have summoned European conferences, set up various organizations for the unification of Europe, created a Council of Europe composed of a Consultative Assembly and a Council of Ministers. With a view to achieving military integration they conceived the Brussels Pact which has given birth to a Western union subsequently transformed into the Western European Union thanks to the participation of the German Federal Republic. [Furthermore], various European states have signed the North Atlantic Pact and joined NATO. Thus, under cover of the 'unification' of Europe, the imperialist promoters of integration have divided Europe into economic, political and military groups opposed to one another; they have created an aggressive military bloc of Western European powers aimed against the Soviet Union and the popular democracies. All these measures have been taken mostly on the initiative, and in every case with the active support, of the ruling circles of the United States who are the leaders of the imperialist camp. . . .

3. Who inspired these agreements on the economic 'union' of Europe? Which classes and social groups will benefit from the realization of the plans for a Common Market, Euratom and

Eurafrica? Behind the six governments which signed the Treaties of Rome are the monopolies in each of these countries. These six countries form a group of developed capitalist states with a high degree of industrial concentration and of capital centralization, and a powerful financial oligarchy at their disposal. The process of fusion of monopolies with the state characterizes all these states. This explains why the agreements on the Common Market, Euratom and Eurafrica represent in reality an alliance of the most powerful monopolies, cartels, and trusts of the industry and banks in these six countries. In no sense have the Six been persuaded to sign these agreements to further the interests of the broad mass of people, whose opinion they did not even consult. . . .

4. What causes lie behind the agreements on the Common Market, Euratom and Eurafrica and to what end have they been concluded? The formation of international unions of monopolies is one of the characteristic traits of imperialism. These unions have precise economic and political aims: the universal struggle for markets, for the sources of raw materials, for possibilities of capital investment; the partition of the world; the safeguarding of the common interests of the class of exploiters; the defence of capital which knows no country. . . . Behind the project for a Common Market and the other measures already taken by the monopolists of the Six lies the desire to unite the forces of imperialism with a view on the one hand to doing battle against socialism and against the movements of national liberation of the colonized peoples and in the lands under their thumb, and on the other hand to consolidate the power of capitalism by resorting to international unions of a governmental and monopolistic kind. . . .

5. . . . The Common Market and Euratom have been created in order to reinforce the economic and military foundations and to extend the activities of the aggressive blocs of imperialist powers. . . .

6. It goes without saying that the promoters and signatories of the Treaties of Rome, instructed by the unhappy experience of the failure of the EDC, have to pretend that these Treaties do not have a supranational character and that they contain nothing which could threaten the sovereign rights of any state. But the language of facts tells otherwise. The Treaties establishing the EEC and Euratom provide for the setting up of various controlling organs (Council of Ministers, Commission, Assembly, etc.). The transference to these institutions of certain important competences in the economic, political and military fields will result in the curtailment of the sovereignty of the weaker states; it will inevitably limit the rights of the Parliaments of these

countries to make important social and national decisions. . . . In transferring, to the detriment of the legislative powers of Member States, certain competences to the supranational organs of the 'Little Europe' and in reinforcing the supranational executive power closely linked to the monopolies, the reactionary circles of the different West European states hope to enfeeble the opposition of the broad mass of people to this aggressive 'Atlantic policy' and to undermine the peoples' struggle for their national sovereignty and the independence of their domestic and foreign policies. . . .

10. The Common Market and Euratom may also have the most baneful consequences for the political rights and democratic liberties of the working class. . . .

11. The Treaty of Rome is also aimed against the interests of the peasantry. Although because of bitter disputes among the imperialists the question of agriculture still remains open, the Treaty of Rome establishes nevertheless a 'special arrangement' for agriculture. In any event the fundamental differences in the agricultural economies of the Six, the wish to lower the costs of production where they are relatively high, the attempts of large-scale capital to make use of the slogan 'agricultural common market' to proceed to a further concentration of agricultural production—all these are prejudicial to the peasantry and the farm workers and threaten to aggravate their situation. . . .

13. The problem of the tariff wall with which the Six plan to surround their Common Market is causing disquiet in the ruling circles of non-member states. Many of them have come out against the Common Market, estimating rightly that this institution will have unfavourable effects on their exports to the Six countries of the 'Little Europe' and will create new obstacles to the development of international economic relations. This position has been adopted by various West European countries, in particular Switzerland, Austria, and the Scandinavian countries. The Japanese claim that the Common Market has declared 'a general tariff war on the rest of the world'. . . .

Editor's translation from B. Dutoit, *L'Union Soviétique face à l'intégration européenne*, 183–207. Lausanne, 1964

32   Statement of Charles de Gaulle at a press conference, 15 May 1962

I would like incidentally, since the opportunity has arisen, to point out to you, gentlemen of the press—and you are perhaps going to be very surprised by this—that I have never personally, in any of my statements, spoken of a 'Europe of nations', although it is always being claimed that I have done so. It is not, of course, that I am repudiating my own; quite on the contrary, I am more attached to France than ever, and I do not believe that Europe can have any living reality if it does not include France and her Frenchmen, Germany and its Germans, Italy and its Italians, and so forth. Dante, Goethe, Chateaubriand belong to all Europe to the very extent that they were respectively and eminently Italian, German and French. They would not have served Europe very well if they had been stateless or if they had thought and written in some kind of integrated Esperanto or Volapük.

But it is true that the nation is a human and sentimental element, whereas Europe can be built on the basis of active, authoritative and responsible elements. What elements? The states, of course; for, in this respect; it is only the states that are valid, legitimate and capable of achievement. I have already said, and I repeat, that at the present time there cannot be any other Europe than a Europe of states, apart, of course, from myths, stories and parades. What is happening with regard to the Economic Community proves this every day, for it is the states, and only the states, that created this Economic Community, that furnished it with funds, that provided it with staff members; and it is the states that give it reality and efficiency, all the more so as it is impossible to take any far-reaching economic measure without committing a political action.

It is a political action when tariffs are dealt with in common, when coalmining areas are converted, when wages and social welfare funds are made the same in the six states, when each state allows workers from the five other states to settle on its territory, when decrees are consequently taken and when Parliament is asked to vote necessary laws, funds and sanctions. It is a political action when agriculture is included in the Common Market, and it is the six states, and they alone, that succeeded in doing so last January by means of their political bodies. It is a political action when the association of Greece or of the African states or of the Malagasy Republic is being dealt with. It is a political action when one negotiates with Great Britain on the request that she has made to enter the Common Market. It is again a political action when the applications of other states for participation or association are considered. It is still a political action when one comes to consider the requests that the United States announces that it will make with regard to its economic relations with the Community.

In fact, the economic development of Europe cannot be assured without its political union and, in this regard, I want to point out the arbitrary nature of a certain idea that was voiced during the recent discussions in Paris and that claimed to keep economic matters out of the meetings of the heads of state or government, whereas, for each of them, in their respective countries, economy is the constant and primary issue.

I should like to speak more particularly about the objection to integration. The objection is presented to us with the words, 'Let us merge the six states into a supranational entity; this way, things will be quite simple and practical.' But such an entity cannot be found without there being in Europe today a federator with sufficient power, authority and skill. That is why one falls back on a type of hybrid, in which the six states would undertake to comply with what will be decided upon by a certain majority. At the same time, although there are already six national parliaments, plus the European Parliament, plus the Consultative Assembly of the Council of Europe—which did, it is ¬rue, predate the conception of the Six and which, I am told, is dying on the shore where it was abandoned—we must, it seems, elect yet another parliament, a so-called European one—which would lay down the law for the six states.

There are ideas that may, perhaps, beguile certain minds, but I certainly do not see how they could be carried out in practice, even if there were six signatures on the dotted line. Is there a France, a Germany, an Italy, a Holland, a Belgium, a Luxembourg, that would be ready—in a matter that is important for them from the national or the international point of view—to do something that they would consider bad because this would be dictated to them by others? Would the French people, the German people, the Italian people, the Dutch people, the Belgian people, or the Luxembourg people dream of submitting to laws voted by foreign deputies if these laws were to run contrary to their own deep-seated will? This is not so; there is no way, at the present time, for a foreign majority to be able to constrain recalcitrant nations. It is true that, in this 'integrated' Europe, as they say, there would perhaps be no policy at all. This would simplify things a great deal. Indeed, once there would be no France and no Europe, once there would be no policy—since no one policy could be imposed on each of the six states—one would refrain from making any policies at all. But then, perhaps, this world would follow the lead of some outsider who did have a policy. There would perhaps be a federator, but the federator would not be European. And it would not be an integrated Europe, it would be something quite different, much broader and much more extensive with, I repeat, a federator. Perhaps it is this which, sometimes and to a certain degree, is at the basis of some remarks of such or such an advocate of European integration. In that case, it would be best to say so.

You see, when one's mind dwells on matters of great import, it is pleasant to dream of the marvellous lamp that Aladdin had only to rub in order to soar above the real. But there is no magic formula that will make it possible to build something as difficult as a united Europe. Thus, let us place reality at the basis of the edifice and, when we shall have completed the work, this will be the time for us to lull ourselves to sleep with the tales of 'The Thousand and One Nights'.

French Embassy Information Bulletin, May 1962

33   Speech of N. S. Khrushchev at the Soviet–Mali friendship meeting, held in the Kremlin, 30 May 1962

. . . Recently the imperialist monopolies have been pinning very great hopes on the so-called Common Market.

The ideologists of imperialism are praising to the skies this organization, extolling the blessings it allegedly offers to its Member States. But their claims are very remote from reality. The Common Market is in fact a state monopoly agreement of the financial oligarchy of Western Europe which is threatening the vital interests of all peoples and the cause of universal peace, since the aggressive circles of imperialism are using it with the aim of strengthening NATO and stepping up the arms race.

The Common Market is also directed against the Soviet Union and other socialist countries. However, our countries have now become such a powerful force that no Common Market is any danger to us. The situation is different for the young states of Asia, Africa and Latin America which have recently gained political independence and have not yet become economically independent.

One of the main purposes of the Common Market is to tie a number of liberated countries to the economy of the imperialist states, to keep them enslaved. This aim, of course, is concealed by high-sounding phrases about 'assistance' to the peoples of the backward countries, about the advantages of selling their goods free of customs duties on the Common Market, etc. . . .

By means of the Common Market the imperialists want to flood the African countries with their manufactured goods, against which, of course, the newly-founded industry of those countries cannot compete. At the same time the imperialist monopolies are seeking to create all kinds of obstacles to the young independent states selling their agri- cultural produce in the markets of Western Europe and America.

Subordination of the young sovereign states of Africa to the Common Market would mean their consent to reconcile themselves to playing the part of agrarian-raw material hinterlands of the former metropolitan countries. But it was not for the sake of this that the African peoples rose in a sacred struggle against colonialism. . . .

The vital interests of the peoples of Asia, Africa and Latin America call for a radical improvement in the system of world trade. It is high time to eliminate from the practice of international trade methods by means of which the strong wax fat from trade with the weak. It is precisely such vicious conditions that constitute the essence of the policy of the Common Market towards the young national states.

The Soviet government believes that the United Nations cannot remain aloof from this question, which is of vital importance for hundreds of millions of people. It considers it desirable to convene an international conference on problems of trade which would discuss the question of setting up an international trade organization to embrace all regions and countries of the world without any discrimination. . . .

We are convinced that the socialist states and the freedom-loving independent countries of Africa, Asia and Latin America can, by their joint efforts, deal a fitting rebuff to the plans of collective colonialism which the imperialists are seeking to implement, taking advantage of the aggressive policy of the Common Market. . . .

Soviet News, 31 May 1962

34 Memorandum of the International Congress of the European Movement on the Political Union of Europe, held in Munich, 7–8 June 1962

The aim of the European Movement remains the creation of a powerful Community in keeping with the contemporary world: the United States of Europe; which must be capable of fulfilling the functions which the nation states acting on their own can no longer exercise. This Community, open to all the democratic countries in Europe which accept its rules, will extend itself to the others as soon as they regain their freedom, or their political evolution permits. Above all it must be able to master all modern technologies so as to derive the maximum advantage from them, to develop them for the security and prosperity of its population, and to achieve more effective collaboration with all other peoples, especially those who are in the process of development. Such an objective will not be achieved until a democratic organization has been established, comprising a European Government, a European Parliament, a Court of Justice and an Economic and Social Council, which respects the human personality, the originality of local communities, and the individuality of each nation. Before the full realization of this Community and in preparation for it, it will be important to develop and strengthen structures which will allow the pursuit of the common interests of the member countries by effecting certain transfers of sovereignty to institutions, independent of the States, which will respect and promote these common interests. To this end, the best technique is that of the Community, already employed in the three Treaties of Paris and Rome, which consists in associating the national governments with a Community organism to which responsibilities are given progressively.

The European Community will only develop if the decisions of governments are inspired by, oriented towards and stimulated by a powerful popular movement. The transition to the second stage of the Common Market is a striking success which raises as many problems as it resolves. At the same time, the recent attempts at a European Union based exclusively on the States have in fact blocked all possibility of progress and also risked putting in question what has happily been achieved. The Munich Congress of the European Movement is concerned to coordinate and galvanize every possible force at this particularly critical moment.

Already within the framework of the existing Treaties, one can and one ought to develop the Europe of the Community. As a matter of urgency its institutions should be reinforced by:

(a) the merging of the High Authority and the Commissions, which should nevertheless conserve intact their existing powers, be delegated substantial new powers by the Council, and see their independence from the Governments reinforced.

(b) the election by direct universal suffrage of a sizeable proportion of the members of the European Parliament which, at the same time, should use its powers with more authority. . . .

(c) the investment of the communities with their own [financial] resources as provided for by the Treaties.

Implementation of the Treaties should be further accelerated; the second and third stages could be shortened.

Common policies should be drawn up and vigorously applied in the spirit of the Treaties to ensure fair competition, the diffusion of economic progress in all the Member States and in every region, the institution of a planned programme to provide harmonized growth and giving priority to the utilization of increases in revenue for social progress. A common currency should be prepared for through closer monetary coordination and the establishment of a [European] money of account. One cannot make Europe without Europeans. The projected creation of a European University must be realized, as well as the development of institutions like the College of Europe [at Bruges] and the European Cultural Centre [at Geneva], both founded by the European Movement, and the Europeanization of national establishments, all of which will allow teachers to work in teams, students to travel in the course of their studies, scholars and young intellectuals to acquire a wider outlook, a better acquaintance with the peoples of Europe, and indeed a more lively feeling of belonging to one and the same community.

The creation of a political Europe, in order to extend the competence of the Community to the fields of diplomacy, defence, and culture . . . is a matter of urgency. It is important to negotiate a multilateral cultural agreement between the Community countries as soon as possible. This implies a new treaty which must not, however, diminish the powers, or modify the structure, or weaken the dynamism, of the Communities; nor those of NATO, that larger and necessary framework of Western defence. . . . Any States which, adhering to the principles governing the three existing European Communities, belong to a free Europe and are true democracies, may form part of this political Europe. The new treaty ought to confer, in one or two stages, new powers as regards foreign policy and defence on the Council of the existing Communities which, meeting at the level of Heads of State or Governments, or of Ministers, will in response to recommendations from a unified Executive, take decisions first unanimously, later by qualified majority. This Executive, independent of the States and representing the general interest of Europe, will have to see to the execution of these decisions. In the exercise of these new powers both Council and Executive must be under the control of the Parliament and the Court of Justice. . . .

Editor's translation from typescript in French
issued by the International Secretariat of the
European Movement, Brussels

35 Speech of J. F. Kennedy in the Paulskirche in Frankfurt, 25 June 1963

One hundred and fifteen years ago a most learned Parliament was convened in this historic hall. Its goal was a united German Federation. Its members were poets and professors, lawyers and philosophers, doctors and clergymen, freely elected in all parts of the land. No nation applauded its endeavours as warmly as my own. No assembly ever strove more ardently to put perfection into practice. And though in the end it failed, no other building in Germany deserves more the title of 'cradle of German democracy.' . . .

For we live in an age of interdependence as well as independence—an age of internationalism as well as nationalism. In 1848 many countries were indifferent to the goals of the Frankfurt Assembly. It was, they said, a German problem. Today there are no exclusively German problems, or American problems, or even European problems. There are world problems—and our two countries and continents are inextricably bound together in the tasks of peace as well as war.

We are partners for peace—not in a narrow bilateral context but in a framework of Atlantic partnership. The ocean divides us less than the Mediterranean divided the ancient world of Greece and Rome. Our Constitution is old and yours is young, and our culture is young and yours is old, but in our commitment we can and must speak and act with but one voice. Our roles are distinct but complementary—and our goals are the same: peace and freedom for all men, for all time, in a world of abundance, in a world of justice.

That is why our nations are working together to strengthen NATO, to expand trade, to assist the developing countries, to align our monetary policies and to build the Atlantic Community. I would not diminish the miracle of West Germany's economic achievements. But the true German miracle has been your rejection of the past for the future—your reconciliation with France, your participation in the building of Europe, your leading role in NATO, and your growing support for constructive undertakings throughout the world.

Your economic institutions, your constitutional guarantees, your confidence in civilian authority, are all harmonious with the ideals of older democracies. And they form a firm pillar of the democratic European Community. . . .

The future of the West lies in Atlantic partnership—a system of cooperation, interdependence, and harmony whose peoples can jointly meet their burdens and opportunities throughout the world. Some say this is only a dream, but I do not agree. A generation of achievement—the Marshall plan, NATO, the Schuman plan, and the Common Market—urges us up the path to greater unity.

There will be difficulties and delays. There will be doubts and discouragement. There will be differences of approach and opinion. But we have the will and the means to serve three related goals–the heritage of our countries, the unity of our continents, and the interdependence of the Western alliance.

Some say that the United States will neither hold to these purposes nor abide by its pledges—that we will revert to a narrow nationalism. But such doubts fly in the face of history. For eighteen years the United States has stood its watch for freedom all around the globe. The firmness of American will, and the effectiveness of American strength, have been shown, in support of free men and free government, in Asia, in Africa, in the Americas, and, above all, here in Europe. We have undertaken, and sustained in honour, relations of mutual trust and obligation with more than forty allies. We are proud of this record, which more than answers doubts. But in addition these proven commitments to the common freedom and safety are assured, in the future as in the past, by one great fundamental fact—that they are deeply rooted in America's own self-interest. Our commitment to Europe is indispensable—in our interest as well as yours.

It is not in our interest to try to dominate the European councils of decision. If that were our objective, we would prefer to see Europe divided and weak, enabling the United States to deal with each fragment individually. Instead we have and now look forward to a Europe united and strong—speaking with a common voice—acting with a common will—a world power capable of meeting world problems as a full and equal partner.

This is in the interest of us all. For war in Europe, as we learned twice in forty years, destroys peace in America. A threat to the freedom of Europe is a threat to the freedom of America. That is why no administration—no administration—in Washington can fail to respond to such a threat—not merely from good will but from necessity. And that is why we look forward to a united Europe in an Atlantic partnership—an entity of interdependent parts, sharing equally both burdens and decisions, and linked together in the tasks of defence as well as the arts of peace. . . .

The great present task of construction is here on this continent where the effort for a unified free Europe is under way. It is not for Americans to prescribe to Europeans how this effort should be carried forward. Nor do I believe that there is any one right course or any single final pattern. It is Europeans who are building Europe.

Yet the reunion of Europe, as Europeans shape it—bringing a permanent end to the civil wars that have repeatedly racked the world—will continue to have the determined support of the United States. For that reunion is a necessary step in strengthening the community of freedom. It would strengthen our alliance for its defence. And it would be in our national interest as well as yours.

It is only a fully cohesive Europe that can protect us all against the fragmentation of our alliance. Only such a Europe will permit full reciprocity of treatment across the ocean, in facing the Atlantic agenda. With only such a Europe can we have a full give-and-take between equals, an equal sharing of responsibilities, and an equal level of sacrifice. I repeat again—so that there may be no misunderstanding—the choice of paths to the unity of Europe is a choice which Europe must make. But as you continue this great effort, undeterred by either difficulty or delay, you should know that this new European greatness will be not an object of fear, but a source of strength, for the United States of America. . . .

Public papers of the Presidents of the USA. John F. Kennedy, 1963, no. 266. Washington, 1964

36 Declaration of the socialist parties of the EEC countries on the Franco–German Treaty, 14 March 1963

The reconciliation of the peoples of Germany and France had always been a major preoccupation of European social democrats, but this could not be achieved by returning to a classical system of alliances. The common aim was therefore to establish an indissoluble union of the essential interests of the European peoples in place of centuries-long rivalries. The reconciliation of the German and French peoples had to act as a catalyst towards the creation of a community of all the European peoples, who had been divided for a long time by bloody rivalries. This aim could not be reached without limiting the sovereignty of the nation states; nor could it be realized by the establishment of any sort of hegemony. Thus the reconciliation of the German and French peoples has been a means and an end of the creation of the European Community, to the realization of which socialists have made a substantial contribution. The creation of the ECSC, the Common Market and Euratom is seen by socialists only as a preliminary to the United States of Europe. Within this multilateral framework the reconciliation of the peoples was already on the way to fulfilment before the Franco–German treaty of bilateral cooperation between the two states was signed in Paris on 22 January 1963. This reconciliation was already present before nationalistic tendencies, which threaten to weaken and even shatter the integration so far achieved, began once again to be promoted in Europe. Therefore the Liaison Office of the socialist parties of the EEC countries is of the following opinion:

1. All the aims of the Franco–German Treaty could have been achieved more effectively in the framework and with the methods of the wider European Community.

2. In its existing form this Treaty endangers the trust between the partners of the European Community. It disquiets the other Member States by suggesting an intention to set up a hegemony, and in consequence risks undermining European solidarity.

3. It endangers the mechanism of reaching majority decisions within the European Community by making possible prior understandings between two governments on matters belonging to the competence of the Community. The consultation procedure laid down in the Treaty thus introduces the danger of paralysing the functioning of the institutions of the European Community.

4. Its methods, which are inspired by the outworn concept of the absolute sovereignty of states, constitute a return to a system of alliance the dangers of which have been demonstrated by two World Wars. In no way does this treaty represent a contribution to the realization of the United States of Europe. . . .

> Editor's translation from French text issued by the Liaison Office of the Socialist Parties of the Member States of the European Community and the Socialist Group of the European Parliament

VII

The Common Market since 1960

The documents grouped in this final chapter illustrate above all the uncertain pace of European integration in the last fifteen years: draft treaties never implemented rather than treaties signed and ratified, and, most noticeable, the high-sounding, all-embracing, verbose declarations agreed to by the Heads of State at those 'Summit Meetings' which, since the first was held in Paris on 10 and 11 February 1961, have tended to transform the activities or progress of the Common Market into a series of whiffs of hot air. The Communiqués of those of 1969 and 1974 are included here (40 and 44) and the reader can judge for himself how much talk and how little action there has been in the years between them.

The plans for a political union of European powers and for a directly elected European Parliament—in place of existing Assemblies which simply consist of Members appointed from the national Parliaments—which had been put forward in the 1962 Memorandum of the European Movement (34) were easily drafted in the form of treaties (37 and 38); and then just as easily shelved. To this day, twelve or fifteen years later, neither has been implemented, though the directly elected European Parliament has been promised for 1978. Whereas the original 1962 plan was based on a report by a Belgian Member, Fernand Dehousse, the revised convention, which was debated and passed in the European Parliament on 14 January 1975, envisaging a Parliament of 355 Members with numbers weighted somewhat in favour of the smaller powers, was drawn up by the Dutch socialist MP Schelto Patijn. Both in 1962 and 1975 the European Parliament was only doing its best to implement Article 138 (3) of the Treaty of Rome. It now remains for the Council of Ministers to do what it failed to do in 1962, and vote unanimously in favour of the project; but the reservations of the Danish and British governments, expressed in the December 1974 Summit Meeting communiqué (44) show that this unanimity is by no means inevitable.

The Fouchet Plan of 1961 (38), so called because the six-nation Commission appointed after the February 1961 Summit Meeting to draw it up elected the head of the French delegation, Christian Fouchet, as its Chairman, represented a Gaullist, confederal and intergovernmental revival of the scheme for a European Political Community which had been shelved in 1954. It too was dropped, and the idea of a political union of some kind was not seriously revived until, more than ten years later, the Summit Meeting of October 1972 declared at the end of its communiqué with masterly imprecision, that: 'The Heads of State or Government, having set themselves the major objective of transforming, before the end of the present decade and with the fullest respect for the treaties already signed, the whole complex of the relations of Member States into a European union, request the institutions of the Community to draw up a report on this subject before the end of 1975 for submission to a summit conference.' Two years later, after no progress had been made, the December 1974 Summit Meeting was only slightly more definite (44); but at least the Belgian Prime Minister M. Tindemans did, in January 1976, submit his 'comprehensive report' on 'European union'.

If in 1965, after prolonged disputes and delays, the 'merging of the executives' of the Communities was finally settled on, their subordination to national interests was conceded in the Luxembourg agreements early in 1966 (39). Among these setbacks, the statement of the Commission of the EEC in July 1968 recording the complete abolition of customs duties inside the Common Market eighteen months ahead of schedule, shone like a beacon. But more significant by far in the eyes of history will probably prove to be the enlargement of the Community provided for in the Treaty of Accession of 1972 (41), even though Norway in the event stayed outside, and Britain only confirmed her membership after renegotiation and the referendum of 6 June 1975 (45). Nevertheless, it seems likely that, from 1972 onwards, there will have been a steadily increasing identification of European integration in the West with the EEC. That is to say, that most future official or 'governmental' integration will probably be inside the Common Market. This, of course, will not prevent convinced neutrals from remaining aloof; nor does it prevent a non-member country like Norway from establishing a close and profitable relationship with the Community (42). Lastly, we have included a reminder that it is no use pretending that membership of an international or supranational (there is some verbal quibbling here as well as some real distinction) organization like the Common Market makes no incursion on our national identity (43): long-standing national laws are being everywhere modified by the operation of the Treaty of Rome.

37   Resolution embodying a draft Convention on the election of the European Parliamentary Assembly by direct universal suffrage, 17 May 1960

The European Parliamentary Assembly:
  considering that the time has come to bring the peoples of Europe into direct association in the task of European construction,
  aware that an Assembly elected on a basis of direct universal suffrage is likely to be an essential element in the pattern of European unification,
  in implementation of the mandate conferred on it by the treaties establishing the European Communities,
  approves the following text of a draft Convention.

Article 1

The representatives of the peoples in the European Parliamentary Assembly shall be elected direct by universal suffrage.

Article 2

The number of Representatives elected in each Member State will be fixed as follows:

Belgium	42
Germany	108
France	108
Italy	108
Luxembourg	18
Netherlands	42

Article 3

During a transitional period one-third of these Representatives will be elected by the Member Parliaments in accordance with a mode of procedure designed to ensure equitable representation for the several political groups.

Article 4

The transitional period will run from the date of the entry into force of this Convention.

The end-date will be fixed by the European Parliamentary Assembly. It cannot be before the end of the third stage of the establishment of the common market, as prescribed in Article 8 of the Treaty establishing the EEC, it cannot be after the expiry of the legislative period marking the end of that third stage.

Article 5

1. The Representatives shall be elected for five years.

Nevertheless, the mandate of the Representatives elected by the Parliaments shall lapse if a member ceases to sit in his national Parliament or, alternatively, at the end of the period for which they have been elected by their respective Parliaments. Any Representative whose mandate comes to an end in this way shall remain a member until his successor's credentials have been confirmed by the European Parliamentary Assembly.

2. The five years period of a legislature shall begin to run from the opening of the first session to be held after the election.

Article 6

Representatives shall vote individually and personally. They shall not receive instructions nor shall they take orders from anyone.

Article 7

During the transitional period the status of Representative to the European Parliamentary Assembly will be compatible with that of a national Member of Parliament.

The Assembly will decide if the two functions are still compatible after the end of the transitional period. . . .

Article 9

The European Parliamentary Assembly shall fix the rules governing, with the maximum possible uniformity, the election of Representatives at the conclusion of the transitional period mentioned in Article 4.

Until such provisions come into force the electoral régime will remain within the competence of each Member State, subject to the provisions of the present Convention.

Article 10

The electorate in each Member State, subject to the provisions of Article 11, shall consist of those persons, male and female, who satisfy

the necessary conditions in each State for participation in elections by
direct universal suffrage for the designation of its Parliament.

Article 11

The age for the exercise of the right of vote shall be twenty-one
years. . . .

Article 14

Elections for the European Parliamentary Assembly will take place
on the same day in the six Member States; the date will be fixed so as
not to coincide with national elections.

Notwithstanding, for reasons connected with tradition or
geography any Member State may decide that the voting operations
take place on the day before or the day after the scheduled date, or may
be spread over the two days.

European yearbook 8 : 487–95. The Hague, 1960

38   The Fouchet Plan for a European political union: draft treaty of 2 November 1961

THE HIGH CONTRACTING PARTIES

Convinced that the organization of Europe in a spirit of freedom that
respects its diversity will enable their civilization to develop still
further, protect their common spiritual heritage from any threats to
which it may be exposed and in this way contribute to the maintenance
of peaceful relations in the world;

Resolved jointly to safeguard the fundamental dignity, freedom and
equality of men, regardless of their status, race or creed, and to work
for the advent of a better world in which these values would
permanently prevail;

Affirming their attachment to the principles of democracy, to the
rights of man and to justice in every sphere of social life;

Desirous of welcoming to their ranks the other countries of Europe
that are prepared to accept the same responsibilities and the same
obligations;

Resolved to pursue the task of reconciling their essential interests,
already the objective, in their respective fields, of the ECSC, EEC and
Euratom, in order to lay the foundation for a destiny to be henceforth
irrevocably shared;

Resolved, to this end, to give statutory form to the union of their peoples, in accordance with the declaration adopted in Bonn on 18 July 1961 by the Heads of State or Government;

have appointed as their plenipotentiaries:

....

who, having exchanged their Full Powers, found in good and due form, have agreed as follows:

UNION OF THE EUROPEAN PEOPLES

Article 1

By the present Treaty, a union of States, hereafter called 'the Union', is established.

The Union is based on respect for the individuality of the peoples and of the Member States and for equality of rights and obligations. It is indissoluble.

Article 2

It shall be the aim of the Union:

to bring about the adoption of a common foreign policy in matters that are of common interest to Member States;

to ensure, through close cooperation between Member States in the scientific and cultural field, the continued development of their common heritage and the protection of the values on which their civilization rests;

to contribute thus in the Member States to the defence of human rights, the fundamental freedoms and democracy;

to strengthen, in cooperation with the other free nations, the security of Member States against any aggression by adopting a common defence policy.

Article 3

The Union shall have legal personality.

The Union shall enjoy in each of the Member States the most extensive legal capacity accorded to legal persons under their domestic law. It may, in particular, acquire or dispose of movable or immovable property and may go to law.

INSTITUTIONS OF THE UNION

Article 4

The Institutions of the Union shall be as follows:

the Council.
the European Parliament.
the European Political Commission

Article 5

The Council shall meet every four months at Head of State or Government level, and at least once in the intervening period at Foreign Minister level. It may, moreover, at any time hold extraordinary sessions at either level at the request of one or more Member States.

At each of these meetings at Head of State or Government level, the Council shall appoint a President who shall take up his duties two months before the subsequent meeting and continue to exercise them for two months after the meeting.

Meetings of the Council held at Foreign Minister level shall be presided over by the Foreign Minister of the State whose representative presides over meetings at Head of State or Government level.

The President in office shall preside over extraordinary meetings that may be held during his term of office.

The Council shall choose the place for its meetings.

Article 6

The Council shall deliberate on all questions whose inclusion on its agenda is requested by one or more Member States. It shall adopt decisions necessary for achieving the aims of the Union unanimously. The absence or abstention of one or of two members shall not prevent a decision from being taken.

The decisions of the Council shall be binding on Member States that have participated in their adoption. Member States on which a decision is not binding, by reason of their absence or abstention, may endorse it at any time. From the moment they endorse it, the decision will be binding on them.

Article 7

The European Parliament provided for under Article 1 of the Convention relating to certain institutions common to the European

Communities signed in Rome on 25 March 1957, shall deliberate on matters concerning the aims of the Union.

It may address oral or written questions to the Council.

It may submit recommendations to the Council.

Article 8

The Council, on receipt of a question addressed to it by the European Parliament, shall give its reply to the Parliament within a period of four months.

The Council, on the receipt of a recommendation addressed to it by the European Parliament, shall inform the Parliament of the action it has taken thereon within a period of six months.

The Council shall each year submit to the European Parliament a report on its activities.

Article 9

The European Political Commission shall consist of senior officials of the Foreign Affairs departments of each Member State. Its seat shall be in Paris. It shall be presided over by the representative of the Member State that presides over the Council, and for the same period.

The European Political Commission shall set up such working bodies as it considers necessary.

The European Political Commission shall have at its disposal the staff and departments it requires to carry out its duties.

Article 10

The European Political Commission shall assist the Council. It shall prepare its deliberations and carry out its decisions. It shall perform the duties that the Council decides to entrust to it.

OBLIGATIONS OF MEMBER STATES

Article 11

There shall be solidarity, mutual confidence and reciprocal assistance as between Member States. They undertake to abstain from any step or decision that might hinder or delay the achievement of the aims of the Union. They shall loyally cooperate in any consultations proposed to them and respond to requests for information addressed to them by the Council or, in compliance with the instructions of the Council, by the European Political Commission.

FINANCES OF THE UNION

Article 12

The budget of the Union shall be drawn up by the Council each year and shall include all revenues and expenditures.

Article 13

The revenues of the Union shall be derived from contributions by the Member States calculated according to the following scale:

Belgium	7·9
France	28
Federal Republic of Germany	28
Italy	28
Luxembourg	0·2
Netherlands	7·9
	100·0

Article 14

The budget shall be implemented by the European Political Commission which may delegate to its chairman all or part of the powers necessary for the purpose.

GENERAL PROVISIONS

Article 15

The present Treaty may be reviewed. Draft amendments shall be submitted to the Council by Member States. The Council shall pronounce on such drafts and decide whether or not they should be passed on for an opinion to the European Parliament.

Draft amendments adopted unanimously by the Council shall be submitted for ratification by the Member States, after the European Parliament, where appropriate, has expressed its opinion. They shall come into force once all the Member States have ratified them.

Article 16

Three years after this Treaty comes into force, it shall be subjected to a general review with a view to considering suitable measures for strengthening the Union in the light of the progress already made.

The main objects of such a review shall be the introduction of a unified foreign policy and the gradual establishment of an organization centralizing, within the Union, the European Communities referred to in the Preamble to the present Treaty.

The amendments arising from this review shall be adopted in accordance with the procedure outlined in Article 15 above.

Article 17

The Union shall be open for membership to Member States of the Council of Europe that accept the aims set out in Article 2 above and that have previously acceded to the European Communities referred to in the Preamble to this Treaty.

The admission of a new Member State shall be decided unanimously by the Council after an additional Act to this Treaty has been drawn up. This Act shall contain the necessary adjustments to the Treaty. It shall come into force once the State concerned has submitted its instrument of ratification.

Article 18

This Treaty, drawn up in a single original in the Dutch, French, German and Italian languages, all four texts being equally authentic, shall be deposited in the archives of the Government of. . . . which shall transmit a certified copy to each of the Governments of the other signatory States.

This Treaty shall be ratified. The instruments of ratification shall be deposited with. . . . which shall notify the Governments of the other Member States that this has been done.

This Treaty shall come into force on the day when the instrument of ratification is deposited by the last signatory State to do so.

In witness thereof, the undersigned Plenipotentiaries have affixed their signatures below this Treaty under their common seal.

> *Towards political union. A selection of documents*, European Parliament, Political Committee, 1974, pp. II–XXVIII

39 The Luxembourg agreements, made by the Council of Ministers of the EEC, 29 January 1966

(a) *Relations between the Commission and the Council*

Close cooperation between the Council and the Commission is essential for the functioning and development of the Community.

In order to improve and strengthen this cooperation at every level, the Council considers that the following practical methods of cooperation should be applied, these methods to be adopted by joint agreement, on the basis of Article 162 of the EEC Treaty, without compromising the respective competences and powers of the two Institutes.

1. Before adopting any particularly important proposal, it is desirable that the Commission should take up the appropriate contacts with the Governments of the Member States, through the Permanent Representatives, without this procedure compromising the right of initiative which the Commission derives from the Treaty.

2. Proposals and any other official acts which the Commission submits to the Council and to the Member States are not to be made public until the recipients have had formal notice of them and are in possession of the texts.

The Official Journal should be arranged so as to show clearly which acts are of binding force. The methods to be employed for publishing those texts whose publication is required will be adopted in the context of the current work on the reorganization of the Official Journal.

3. The credentials of Heads of Missions of non-member states accredited to the Community will be submitted jointly to the President of the Council and to the President of the Commission, meeting together for this purpose.

4. The Council and the Commission will inform each other rapidly and fully of any approaches relating to fundamental questions made to either institution by the representatives of non-member states.

5. Within the scope of application of Article 162, the Council and the Commission will consult together on the advisability of, the procedure for, and the nature of any links which the Commission might establish with international organizations pursuant to Article 229 of the Treaty.

6. Cooperation between the Council and the Commission on the Community's information policy, which was the subject of the Council's discussions on 24 September 1963, will be strengthened in such a way that the programme of the Joint Information Service will be drawn up and carried out in accordance with procedures which are to be decided upon at a later date, and which may include the establishment of an *ad hoc* body.

7. Within the framework of the financial regulations relating to the drawing up and execution of the Communities' budgets, the Council

and the Commission will decide on means for more effective control over the commitment and expenditure of Community funds.

(b) *Majority voting procedure*

1. Where, in the case of decisions which may be taken by majority vote on a proposal of the Commission, very important interests of one or more partners are at stake, the Members of the Council will endeavour, within a reasonable time, to reach solutions which can be adopted by all the Members of the Council while respecting their mutual interests and those of the Community, in accordance with Article 2 of the Treaty.

2. With regard to the preceding paragraph, the French delegation considers that where very important interests are at stake the discussion must be continued until unanimous agreement is reached.

3. The six delegations note that there is a divergence of views on what should be done in the event of a failure to reach complete agreement.

4. The six delegations nevertheless consider that this divergence does not prevent the Community's work being resumed in accordance with the normal procedure.

Sweet and Maxwell's European Community
Treaties, 234–5. London, 1972

40 Communiqué issued by the EEC Heads of State, 2 December 1969

1. On the initiative of the Government of the French Republic and at the invitation of the Netherlands Government, the heads of State or Government and the Ministers for Foreign Affairs of the Member States of the European Communities met at the Hague on December 1 and 2, 1969. The Commission of the European Communities was invited to participate in the work of the conference on the second day.

2. Now that the Common Market is about to enter upon its final stage, they considered that it was the duty of those who bear the highest political responsibility in each of the Member States to draw up a balance-sheet of the work already accomplished, to show their determination to continue it and to define the broad lines for the future.

3. Looking back on the road that has been traversed, and finding that never before have independent States pushed their cooperation further, they were unanimous in their opinion that by reason of the

progress made, the Community has now arrived at a turning point in its history. Over and above the technical and legal sides of the problems involved, the expiry of the transitional period at the end of the year has, therefore, acquired major political significance. Entry upon the final stage of the Common Market not only means confirming the irreversible nature of the work accomplished by the Communities, but also means paving the way for a united Europe capable of assuming its responsibilities in the world of tomorrow and of making a contribution commensurate with its traditions and its mission.

4. The Heads of State or Government therefore wish to reaffirm their belief in the political objectives which give the Community its meaning and purport, their determination to carry their undertaking through to the end, and their confidence in the final success of their efforts. Indeed, they have a common conviction that a Europe composed of States which, in spite of their different national characteristics, are united in their essential interests, assured of its internal cohesion, true to its friendly relations with outside countries, conscious of the role it has to play in promoting the relaxation of international tension and the rapprochement among all peoples, and first and foremost among those of the entire European continent, is indispensable if a mainspring of development, progress and culture, world equilibrium and peace is to be preserved.

The European Communities remain the original nucleus from which European unity has been developed and intensified. The entry of other countries of this continent to the Communities—in accordance with the provisions of the Treaties of Rome—would undoubtedly help the Communities to grow in dimensions more in conformity with the present state of world economy and technology.

The creation of a special relationship with other European states which have expressed a desire to that effect would also contribute to this end. A development such as this would enable Europe to remain faithful to its traditions of being open to the world and increase its efforts on behalf of developing countries.

5. As regards the completion of the Communities, the Heads of State or Government reaffirmed the will of their Governments to pass from the transitional period to the final stage of the European Community and, accordingly, to lay down a definitive financial arrangement for the Common Agricultural Policy by the end of 1969.

They agreed progressively to replace, within the framework of this financial arrangement, the contributions of member countries by their own resources, taking into account all the interests concerned, with the object of achieving in due course the integral financing of the Communities' budgets in accordance with the procedure provided for in Article 201 of the Treaty establishing the EEC and of strengthening the budgetary powers of the European Parliament. The problem of the method of direct elections is still being studied by the Council of Ministers. . . .

8. They reaffirmed their readiness to further the more rapid progress of the later development needed to strengthen the Community and promote its development into an economic union. They are of the opinion that the integration process should result in a Community of stability and growth. To this end they agreed that within the Council, on the basis of the memorandum presented by the Commission on 12 February 1969, and in close collaboration with the latter, a plan in stages should be worked out during 1970 with a view to the creation of an Economic and Monetary Union. The development of monetary cooperation should depend on the harmonization of economic policies.

They agreed to arrange for the investigation of the policy of setting up a European Reserve Fund in which a joint economic and monetary policy would have to result.

9. As regards the technological activity of the Community, they reaffirmed their readiness to continue more intensively the activities of the Community with a view to coordinating and promoting industrial research and development in the principal sectors concerned, in particular by means of common programmes, and to supply the financial means for the purpose.

10. They further agreed on the necessity of making fresh efforts to work out in the near future a research programme for Euratom designed in accordance with the exigencies of modern industrial management, and making it possible to ensure the most effective use of the common research centre.

11. They reaffirmed their interest in the establishment of a European University.

12. The Heads of State or Government acknowledge the desirability of reforming the Social Fund, within the framework of a closely concerted social policy.

13. They reaffirmed their agreement on the principle of the enlargement of the Community, as provided by Article 237 of the Treaty of Rome.

In so far as the applicant states accept the treaties and their political

finality, the decisions taken since the entry into force of the treaties and
the options made in the sphere of development, the Heads of State or
Government have indicated their agreement to the opening of
negotiations between the Community on the one hand and the
applicant states on the other.

They agreed that the essential preparatory work could be
undertaken as soon as practically and conveniently possible. By
common consent, the preparations would take place in a most positive
spirit.

14. As soon as negotiations with the applicant countries have been
opened, discussion will be started with such other EFTA members as
may request them on their position in relation to the EEC.

15. They agreed to instruct the Ministers for Foreign Affairs to
study the best way of achieving progress in the matter of political
unification, within the context of enlargement. The Ministers would be
expected to report before the end of July 1970.

16. All the creative activities and the actions conducive to European
growth decided upon here will be assured of a better future if the
younger generation is closely associated with them. The Governments
are resolved to endorse this and the Communities will make provision
for it.

European Community, Dec. 1969, p. 24

41 Treaty concerning the accession of Denmark, Ireland, Norway
and the United Kingdom to the EEC, 22 January 1972

His Majesty the King of the Belgians, Her Majesty the Queen of
Denmark, the President of the Federal Republic of Germany, the
President of the French Republic, the President of Ireland, the
President of the Italian Republic, His Royal Highness the Grand Duke
of Luxembourg, Her Majesty the Queen of the Netherlands, His
Majesty the King of Norway, Her Majesty the Queen of the United
Kingdom of Great Britain and Northern Ireland,

United in their desire to pursue the attainment of the objectives of
the Treaty establishing the EEC and the Treaty establishing Euratom,

Determined in the spirit of those Treaties to construct an ever closer
union among the peoples of Europe on the foundations already laid,

Considering that Article 237 of the Treaty establishing the EEC and
Article 205 of the Treaty establishing Euratom afford European States
the opportunity of becoming members of these Communities,

Considering that the Kingdom of Denmark, Ireland, the Kingdom of Norway and the United Kingdom of Great Britain and Northern Ireland have applied to become members of these Communities,

Considering that the Council of the European Communities, after having obtained the Opinion of the Commission, has declared itself in favour of the admission of these States,

Have decided to establish by common agreement the conditions of admission and the adjustments to be made to the Treaties establishing the EEC and Euratom, and to this end have designated as their Plenipotentiaries: [the names follow].

Who, having exchanged their Full Powers found in good and due form, have agreed as follows:

Article 1

1. The Kingdom of Denmark, Ireland, the Kingdom of Norway and the United Kingdom of Great Britain and Northern Ireland hereby become members of the EEC and of Euratom and Parties to the Treaties establishing these Communities as amended or supplemented.

2. The conditions of admission and the adjustments to the Treaties establishing the EEC and Euratom necessitated thereby are set out in the Act annexed to this Treaty. The provisions of that Act concerning the EEC and Euratom shall form an integral part of this Treaty.

3. The provisions concerning the rights and obligations of the Member States and the powers and jurisdiction of the institutions of the Communities as set out in the Treaties referred to in paragraph 1 shall apply in respect of this Treaty.

Article 2

This Treaty will be ratified by the High Contracting Parties in accordance with their respective constitutional requirements. The instruments of ratification will be deposited with the Government of the Italian Republic by 31 December 1972 at the latest.

This Treaty will enter into force on 1 January 1973, provided that all the instruments of ratification have been deposited before that date and that all the instruments of accession to the ECSC are deposited on that date.

Act concerning the conditions of accession and the adjustments to the Treaties

Article 2

... From the date of accession, the provisions of the original Treaties and the acts adopted by the institutions of the Communities shall be binding on the new Member States and shall apply in those States under the conditions laid down in those Treaties and in this Act.

Article 3

1. The new Member States accede by this Act to the decisions and agreements adopted by the Representatives of the Governments of the Member States meeting in Council. They undertake to accede from the date of accession to all other agreements concluded by the original Member States relating to the functioning of the Communities or connected with their activities. . . .

Article 4

1. The agreements or conventions entered into by any of the Communities with one or more third States, with an international organization or with a national of a third State, shall under the conditions laid down in the original Treaties and in this Act, be binding on the new Member States. . . .

Article 9

1. In order to facilitate the adjustment of the new Member States to the rules in force within the Communities, the application of the original Treaties and acts adopted by the institutions shall, as a transitional measure, be subject to the derogations provided for in this Act.

2. Subject to the dates, time limits and special provisions provided for in this Act, the application of the transitional measures shall terminate at the end of 1977.

Cmnd. 4862–I. London, HMSO

42   Agreement between the EEC and Norway, 14 May 1973

The European Economic Community of the one part, and The Kingdom of Norway of the other part,

Desiring to consolidate and to extend, upon the enlargement of the EEC, the economic relations existing between the Community and Norway and to ensure, with due regard for fair conditions of competition, the harmonious development of their commerce for the purpose of contributing to the work of constructing Europe,

Resolved to this end to eliminate progressively the obstacles to substantially all their trade, in accordance with the provisions of the GATT concerning the establishment of free trade areas,

Declaring their readiness to examine, in the light of any relevant factor, and in particular of developments in the Community, the possibility of developing and deepening their relations where it would appear to be useful in the interests of their economies to extend them to fields not covered by this Agreement,

Have decided, in pursuit of these objectives and considering that no provision of this Agreement may be interpreted as exempting the Contracting Parties from the obligations which are incumbent upon them under other international agreements, to conclude this Agreement:

Article 1

The aim of this Agreement is:

(a) to promote through the expansion of reciprocal trade the harmonious development of economic relations between the EEC and the Kingdom of Norway and thus to foster in the Community and in Norway the advance of economic activity, the improvement of living and employment conditions, and increased productivity and financial stability,

(b) to provide fair conditions of competition for trade between the Contracting Parties,

(c) to contribute in this way, by the removal of barriers to trade, to the harmonious development and expansion of world trade.

Article 2

The Agreement shall apply to products originating in the Community or Norway.

(i) which fall within Chapters 25 to 99 of the Brussels Nomenclature excluding the products listed in the Annex;

(ii) which are specified in Protocol No 2, with due regard to the arrangements provided for in that Protocol.

Article 3

1. No new customs duty on imports shall be introduced in trade between the Community and Norway.

2. Customs duties on imports shall be progressively abolished in accordance with the following timetable:

(a) on the date of entry into force of the Agreement each duty shall be reduced to 80% of the basic duty;
(b) four further reductions of 20% each shall be made on:

1 January 1974
1 January 1975
1 January 1976
1 July 1977.

Article 4

1. The provisions concerning the progressive abolition of customs duties on imports shall also apply to customs duties of a fiscal nature.

The Contracting Parties may replace a customs duty of a fiscal nature or the fiscal element of a customs duty by an internal tax.

2. Denmark, Ireland and the United Kingdom may retain until 1 January 1976 a customs duty of a fiscal nature or the fiscal element of a customs duty in the event of implementation of Article 38 of the «Act concerning the Conditions of Accession and the Adjustments to the Treaties» signed on 22 January 1972.

3. Norway may retain temporarily and not beyond 31 December 1975, while observing the conditions of Article 18, a customs duty of a fiscal nature or the fiscal element of any such duty. . . .

Article 6

1. No new charge having an effect equivalent to a customs duty on imports shall be introduced in trade between the Community and Norway. . . .

Article 7

No customs duty on exports or charge having equivalent effect shall be introduced in trade between the Community and Norway.

Customs duties on exports and charges having equivalent effect shall be abolished not later than 1 January 1974. . . .

Article 13

1. No new quantitative restriction on imports or measures having equivalent effect shall be introduced in trade between the Community and Norway.

2. Quantitative restrictions on imports shall be abolished on the date of entry into force of the Agreement and any measures having an

effect equivalent to quantitative restrictions on imports shall be abolished not later than 1 January 1975. . . .

Article 15

1. The Contracting Parties declare their readiness to foster, so far as their agricultural policies allow, the harmonious development of trade in agricultural products to which the Agreement does not apply.

2. The Contracting Parties shall apply their agricultural rules in veterinary, health and plant health matters in a non-discriminatory fashion and shall not introduce any new measures that have the effect of unduly obstructing trade.

3. The Contracting Parties shall examine . . . any difficulties that might arise in their trade in agricultural products and shall endeavour to seek appropriate solutions.

Article 16

From 1 July 1977 products originating in Norway may not enjoy more favourable treatment when imported into the Community than that applied by the Member States of the Community between themselves.

Article 17

The Agreement shall not preclude the maintenance or establishment of customs unions, free trade areas or arrangements for frontier trade, except insofar as they alter the trade arrangements provided for in the Agreement, in particular the provisions concerning rules of origin.

Article 18

The Contracting Parties shall refrain from any measure or practice of an internal fiscal nature establishing, whether directly or indirectly, discrimination between the products of one Contracting Party and like products originating in the territory of the other Contracting Party.

Products exported to the territory of one of the Contracting Parties may not benefit from repayment of internal taxation in excess of the amount of direct or indirect taxation imposed on them. . . .

Article 29

1. A Joint Committee is hereby established, which shall be responsible for the administration of the Agreement and shall ensure its proper implementation. For this purpose, it shall make

recommendations and take decisions in the cases provided for in the Agreement. These decisions shall be put into effect by the Contracting Parties in accordance with their own rules.

2. For the purpose of the proper implementation of the Agreement the Contracting Parties shall exchange information and, at the request of either Party, shall hold consultations within the Joint Committee.

3. The Joint Committee shall adopt its own rules of procedure.

Article 30

1. The Joint Committee shall consist of representatives of the Community, on the one hand, and of representatives of Norway on the other.

2. The Joint Committee shall act by mutual agreement. . . .

Avtaler mellom Norge og De Europeiske Fellescap,
2–12.   Utenriksdepartementet.   Saerskilt
vedlegg 1 til St. prp. no. 126 for 1972–3

43 Judgement by Lord Denning in the Court of Appeal in the case of Schorsch Meier GmbH v. Hennin, 22 November 1974

Here we see the impact of the Common Market upon our law. No one would have thought of it before. A German company comes to an English court and asks for judgment—not in English pounds sterling, but, if you please, in German Deutschmarks. The judge offered a sterling judgment. But the German company said 'No. Sterling is no good to us. It has gone down much in value. If we accepted it, we would lose one-third of the debt. The debt was payable in Deutschmarks. We want Deutschmarks. We will accept no other.' The judge refused their request. He had no power, he said, in English law to give any judgment but in sterling. The German company appeal to this court.

These are the facts: Schorsch Meier GmbH are dealers in motor car parts and accessories. They have offices and workshops in Munich in the Federal Republic of Germany. Mr Hennin lives in England. He is engaged in the motor car trade. In 1970 and 1971 he ordered spare parts and accessories from the German company. Some of the orders he gave himself when he called at the German company's offices at Munich. Other orders he gave by telephone from England. The company invoiced the goods to him, giving the price in Deutschmarks, and despatched them to him in England. He made some payments in cash when he was in Munich. He made those payments in

Deutschmark bank notes. He also gave two cheques in sterling; but they were dishonoured. On February 3 1972, the German company rendered a statement of account to him. It was for DM 3,756·03 for goods sold and delivered.

The currency of the contract was clearly German. The money of account and the money of payment was German Deutschmarks. At the time when the sum became due the rate of exchange was £1 = DM8·30. At that rate the sterling equivalent of DM3,756·03 was £452 sterling.

Some time later sterling was devalued. As a result £1 sterling was only worth DM5·85.

On July 13 1973, the German company issued a summons in the West London County Court for the sum of DM3,756·03. They claimed the sum in Deutschmarks. They did not claim payment in sterling—and for a very good reason. Sterling had gone down in value. If they had claimed in sterling, they would have had to convert the Deutschmarks into sterling at the date the payment should have been made, that is, February 3 1972: see *In re United Railways of Havana and Regla Warehouses Ltd.* [1961] A.C. 1007. They would have got judgment for only £452, which would at that time have only produced DM2,664; whereas if they were able to claim in Deutschmarks and get judgment in Deutschmarks for DM3,765·03, the sterling equivalent would be £641. In other words, by getting judgment in sterling, they would lose one-third of the money due to them: whereas by getting judgment in Deutschmarks they would recover the full amount.

When the case came before the county court judge, the German company proved the debt owing in Deutschmarks, that is, DM3,765·03. They gave no evidence of rates of exchange. They asked for judgment in Deutschmarks. They relied on the Treaty of Rome. They submitted that the rule of English law (by which an English court can give judgment only in sterling) is incompatible with article 106 of the Treaty. They asked the court to refer the matter to the European Court under Article 177 (a) of the Treaty. The judge refused. He held that, applying English canons of construction, Article 106 had no bearing on the rule of the common law: and that this was so clear that no reference to the European Court was required under Article 177 (a). . . .

So far as I can discover, no one has ever before asked an English court to give judgment in a foreign currency. It has always been assumed that it cannot be done. As long ago as 1605 a merchant sold some cloth to another for 60 Flemish pounds. He brought an action of debt in which he claimed the English equivalent, namely, £39 sterling.

The defendant said he was not indebted in English pounds. The court overruled his objection, and said:

'the debt ought to be demanded by a name known, and the judges are not apprised of Flemish money; and also when the plaintiff has his judgment, he cannot have execution by such name; for the sheriff cannot know how to levy the money in Flemish'. . . .

A few years later this was reaffirmed. In 1626 it was agreed by all the judges that 'in the case of foreign coin, such as Flemish, one must declare the value in English'. . . .

From that time forward it has always been accepted that an English court can only give judgment in sterling. Judges and text book writers have treated it as a self-evident proposition. . . .

Why have we in England insisted on a judgment in sterling and nothing else? It is, I think, because of our faith in sterling. It was a stable currency which had no equal. Things are different now. Sterling floats in the wind. It changes like a weathercock with every gust that blows. So do other currencies. This change compels us to think again about our rules. I ask myself: Why do we say that an English court can only pronounce judgment in sterling? Lord Reid thought that it was 'primarily procedural': see the *Havana* case [1961] A.C. 1007, 1052. I think so too. It arises from the form in which we used to give judgment for money. From time immemorial the courts of common law used to give judgment in these words: 'It is adjudged that the plaintiff *do recover* against the defendant £X' in sterling. On getting such a judgment the plaintiff could at once issue out a writ of execution for £X. If it was not in sterling, the sheriff would not be able to execute it. It was therefore essential that the judgment should be for a sum of money in sterling: for otherwise it could not be enforced. . . .

Those reasons for the rule have now ceased to exist. In the first place, the form of judgment has been altered. In 1966 the common law words 'do recover' were dropped. They were replaced by a simple order that the defendant 'do' the specified act. A judgment for money now simply says that: 'It is [this day] adjudged that the defendant do pay the plaintiff' the sum specified. . . . That form can be used quite appropriately for a sum in foreign currency as for a sum in sterling. It is perfectly legitimate to order the defendant to pay the German debt in Deutschmarks. He can satisfy the judgment by paying the Deutschmarks: or, if he prefers, he can satisfy it by paying the equivalent sum in sterling, that is, the equivalent at the time of payment. . . .

Seeing that the reasons no longer exist, we are at liberty to discard the rule itself. Cessante ratione legis cessat ipsa lex. The rule has no support amongst the juridical writers. . . .

Only last year we refused to apply the rule to arbitrations. We held that English arbitrators have jurisdiction to make their awards in a foreign currency, when that currency is the currency of the contract: see *Jugoslovenska Oceanska Plovidba* v. *Castle Investment Co. Inc.* [1974] Q.B. 292. The time has now come when we should say that when the currency of a contract is a foreign currency—that is to say, when the money of account and the money of payment is a foreign currency—the English courts have power to give judgment in that foreign currency; they can make an order in the form: 'It is adjudged this day that the defendant do pay to the plaintiff so much in foreign currency (being the currency of the contract) 'or the sterling equivalent at the time of payment.' If the defendant does not honour the judgment, the plaintiff can apply for leave to enforce it. He should file an affidavit showing the rate of exchange at the date of the application and give the amount of the debt converted into sterling at that date. Then leave will be given to enforce payment of that sum.

It must be remembered that if the English courts refuse to give a judgment in Deutschmarks, the German company could readily find a way round it. They could bring proceedings in the German courts to get judgment there in Deutschmarks for DM3,756·03. Then they could bring that judgment over to England and register it in the High Court here. On registration here, the sum would have to be converted into sterling 'on the basis of the rate of exchange prevailing at the date of the judgment of the original court'; that is, at the rate in force at the date of the German judgment: see section 2(3) of the Foreign Judgments (Reciprocal Enforcement) Act 1933. By that means the company would get judgment for the full sum they now seek, that is, £641 or thereabouts, and not £452.

I turn now to the Treaty of Rome. It is by statute part of the law of England. It creates rights and obligations, not only between Member States themselves, but also between citizens and the Member States and between the ordinary citizens themselves; and the national courts can enforce those rights and obligations: see *Van Gend en Loos* v. *Nederlandse Tariefcommissie* [1963] C.M.L.R. 105, 129. Whenever the Treaty is prayed in aid, the English courts can themselves interpret it, subject always to the European Court, if asked, having the last word: see *Bulmer (H.P.) Ltd.* v. *J. Bollinger S.A.* [1974] 3 W.L.R. 202 and *Application des Gaz S.A.* v. *Falks Veritas Ltd.* [1974] 3 W.L.R. 235.

Mr Blom-Cooper relies on Article 106 of the Treaty. It says:

'Each Member State undertakes to authorize, *in the currency of the Member State in which the creditor or the beneficiary resides*, any payments connected with the movement of goods, services or capital, and any transfers of capital and earnings, to the extent that the movement of goods and services, capital and persons between Member States has been liberalized pursuant to this Treaty.'

In interpreting this article we need not examine the words in meticulous detail. We have to look at the purpose or intent. . . . There is no need to refer the interpretation to the court at Luxembourg. We can do it ourselves. It seems to me that the purpose of Article 106—or one of its purposes—is to ensure that the creditor in one Member State shall receive payment for his goods in his own currency—if it is the currency of the contract—without any impediment or restriction by reason of changes in the rate of exchange. The underlying principle is this: It is the duty of the debtor to pay his debt to the creditor in the currency of the contract according to its terms. If he delays and sterling depreciates, the creditor ought not to suffer loss as a result of the debtor's delay. The debtor ought to bear the burden of his own default. The English courts would be acting contrary to the spirit and intent of the Treaty if they made a German creditor accept payment in depreciated sterling. In order to comply with the Treaty, they should give judgment that the defendant do pay the stated sum in Deutschmarks or its sterling equivalent at the time of payment. If the defendant fails to comply with that judgment, the plaintiff can apply for leave to enforce it, producing an affidavit showing the sterling equivalent at the date of his application to enforce it. Leave will then be given to enforce payment of that sterling sum.

This is the first case in which we have had actually to apply the Treaty of Rome in these courts. It shows great effect. It has brought about a fundamental change. Hitherto our English courts have only been able to give judgment in sterling. In future when a debt is incurred by an English debtor to a creditor in one of the Member States—payable in the currency of that state—the English courts can give judgment for the amount in that money. This change will have effects, too, beyond the Common Market. It has already made us think again about our own laws. As a result, it is my opinion, that, whatever the foreign currency, be it United States dollars or Japanese yen, or any other, the English courts can give judgment in that money where it is the currency of the contract.

I would allow the appeal and adjudge that the debtor do pay to the
plaintiff DM3,756·03 or the sterling equivalent at the time of payment.

The Weekly Law Reports, 20 December 1974,
823–31 ([1974] 3 W.L.R. 823)

44 Communiqué issued after the Paris meeting of the EEC Heads of State, 10 December 1974

1. The Heads of Government of the nine States of the Community,
the Ministers of Foreign Affairs and the President of the Commission,
meeting in Paris at the invitation of the French President, examined
the various problems confronting Europe. They took note of the
reports drawn up by the Ministers of Foreign Affairs and recorded the
agreement reached by these Ministers on various points raised in the
reports.

2. Recognizing the need for an overall approach to the internal
problems involved in achieving European unity and the external
problems facing Europe, the Heads of Government consider it
essential to ensure progress and overall consistency in the activities of
the Communities and in the work on political cooperation.

3. The Heads of Government have therefore decided to meet,
accompanied by the Ministers of Foreign Affairs, three times a year
and, whenever necessary, in the Council of the Communities and in
the context of political cooperation.

The administrative secretariat will be provided for in an appropriate
manner with due regard for existing practices and procedures.

In order to ensure consistency in Community activites and
continuity of work, the Ministers of Foreign Affairs, meeting in the
Council of the Community, will act as initiators and coordinators.
They may hold political cooperation meetings at the same time.

These arrangements do not in any way affect the rules and
procedures laid down in the Treaties or the provisions on political
cooperation in the Luxembourg and Copenhagen Reports. At the
various meetings referred to in the preceding paragraphs the
Commission will exercise the powers vested in it and play the part
assigned to it by the above texts.

4. With a view to progress towards European unity, the Heads of
Government reaffirm their determination gradually to adopt common
positions and coordinate their diplomatic action in all areas of
international affairs which affect the interests of the European
Community. The President-in-Office will be the spokesman for the

Nine and will set out their views in international diplomacy. He will ensure that the necessary concertation always takes place in good time.

In view of the increasing role of political cooperation in the construction of Europe, the European Assembly must be more closely associated with the work of the Presidency, for example through replies to questions on political cooperation put to him by its Members.

5. The Heads of Government consider it necessary to increase the solidarity of the Nine both by improving Community procedures and by developing new common policies in areas to be decided on and granting the necessary powers to the Institutions.

6. In order to improve the functioning of the Council of the Community, they consider that it is necessary to renounce the practice which consists of making agreement on all questions conditional on the unanimous consent of the Member States, whatever their respective positions may be regarding the conclusions reached in Luxembourg on 28 January 1966.

7. Greater latitude will be given to the Permanent Representatives so that only the most important political problems need be discussed in the Council. To this end, each Member State will take the measures it considers necessary to strengthen the role of the Permanent Representatives and involve them in preparing the national positions on European affairs.

8. Moreover, they agree on the advantage of making use of the provisions of the Treaty of Rome whereby the powers of implementation and management arising out of Community rules may be conferred on the Commission.

9. Cooperation between the Nine in areas outside the scope of the Treaty will be continued where it has already begun. It should be extended to other areas by bringing together the representatives of the Governments, meeting within the Council whenever possible.

10. A working party will be set up to study the possibility of establishing a passport union and, in anticipation of this, the introduction of a uniform passport.

If possible, this draft should be submitted to the Governments of the Member States before 31 December 1976. It will, in particular, provide for stage-by-stage harmonization of legislation affecting aliens and for the abolition of passport control within the Community.

11. Another working party will be instructed to study the conditions and the timing under which the citizens of the nine Member States could be given special rights as members of the Community.

12. The Heads of Government note that the election of the European Assembly by universal suffrage, one of the objectives laid down in the Treaty, should be achieved as soon as possible. In this connection, they await with interest the proposals of the European Assembly, on which they wish the Council to act in 1976. On this assumption, elections by direct universal suffrage could take place at any time in or after 1978.

Since the European Assembly is composed of representatives of the peoples of the States united within the Community, each people must be represented in an appropriate manner.

The European Assembly will be associated with the achievement of European unity. The Heads of Government will not fail to take into consideration the points of view which, in October 1972, they asked it to express on this subject.

The competence of the European Assembly will be extended, in particular by granting it certain powers in the Communities' legislative process.

Statement by the United Kingdom delegation

The Prime Minister of the United Kingdom explained that Her Majesty's Government did not wish to prevent the Governments of the other eight Member States from making progress with the election of the European Assembly by universal suffrage. Her Majesty's Government could not themselves take up a position on the proposal before the process of renegotiation had been completed and the results of renegotiation submitted to the British people.

Statement by the Danish delegation

The Danish delegation is unable at this stage to commit itself to introducing elections by universal suffrage in 1978.

13. The Heads of Government note that the process of transforming the whole complex of relations between the Member States, in accordance with the decision taken in Paris in October 1972, has already started. They are determined to make further progress in this direction.

In this connection, they consider that the time has come for the Nine to agree as soon as possible on an overall concept of European Union. Consequently, in accordance with the requests made by the Paris meeting of Heads of Government in October 1972, they confirm the importance which they attach to the reports to be made by the

Community institutions. They request the European Assembly, the Commission and the Court of Justice to bring the submission of their reports forward to before the end of June 1975. They agreed to invite Mr Tindemans, Prime Minister of the Kingdom of Belgium, to submit a comprehensive report to the Heads of Government before the end of 1975, on the basis of the reports received from the Institutions and of consultations which he is to have with the Governments and with a wide range of public opinion in the Community.

Economic and monetary union

14. The Heads of Government, having noted that internal and international difficulties have prevented in 1973 and 1974 the accomplishment of expected progress on the road to EMU, affirm that in this field their will has not weakened and that their objective has not changed since the Paris Conference.

Convergence of economic policies

15. The Heads of Government discussed the economic situation in the world and in the Community.

16. They noted that the increase in prices is adding to inflationary tendencies and balance of payments deficits and intensifying the threat of general recession. The resulting alterations in the terms of trade are forcing the Member States to redirect their production structures.

17. The Heads of Government reaffirm that the aim of their economic policy continues to be to combat inflation and maintain employment. The cooperation of both sides of industry will be essential if this policy is to succeed. They emphasize that in the present circumstances high priority must be given to economic revival in conditions of stability, i.e. action aimed both at preventing a general economic recession and restoring stability. This must not involve any recourse to protectionist measures which, by setting up a chain reaction, could jeopardize economic revival.

Member States which have a balance of payments surplus must implement an economic policy of stimulating domestic demand and maintaining a high level of employment, without creating new inflationary conditions. Such an attitude would make it easier for countries which have considerable balance of payments deficits to follow a policy which will ensure a satifactory level of employment, stabilization of costs and an improvement in their external trade balance without resorting to protectionist measures.

18. In the context of the effort to be made by countries having a

surplus, the Heads of Government greet the economic policy measures already adopted by the Netherlands Government as a step in the right direction. They also note with satisfaction the short-term economic programme which the Government of the Federal Republic of Germany intends to follow, particularly as regards stimulating public and private investment, and the fact that the Belgian Government intends to follow suit.

They also express satisfaction at the efforts made by the countries having a balance of payments deficit to maintain their competitive position so as to achieve a more satisfactory balance of payments and to improve the level of employment.

19. While acknowledging the special situation of each of the Member States of the Community—which makes a uniform policy inappropriate—the Heads of Government stress that it is absolutely necessary to agree on the policies to be adopted. This convergence will be meaningful only if it works towards Community solidarity and is based on effective permanent consultation machinery. The Ministers for Economic Affairs and Finance will be responsible, within the framework of Community procedures, for implementing these guidelines.

20. It is obvious that all these policies will be really effective only in so far as the world's major industrialized countries succeed in arresting incipient recessionary tendencies.

In this connection, they note with satisfaction the account given by the Chancellor the Federal Republic of Germany of his talks with the President of the United States.

They desire that, at his forthcoming meeting with President Ford, the President of the French Republic should, on behalf of the Community, stress the importance of convergence between the economic policies of all industrialized countries along the lines indicated above.

They also wish the Community and its Member States to do the same during the forthcoming international consultations and in the appropriate internal bodies.

21. The Community will continue to contribute to the harmonious expansion of world trade, especially in relation to developing countries, and in order to do so will take a constructive part in the GATT trade negotiations which it hopes to see actively continued in the near future.

Regional policy

22. The Heads of Government have decided that the European Regional Development Fund, designed to correct the principal regional inbalances in the Community resulting notably from agricultural predominance, industrial change and structural under-employment will be put into operation by the institutions of the Community with effect from 1 January 1975. . . .

Employment problems

25. The effort needed to combat inflation and the risks of recession and unemployment as described above must accord with the imperatives of a progressive and equitable social policy if it is to receive support and cooperation from both sides of industry, both at national and Community level.

In this respect, the Heads of Government emphasize that the Economic and Social Committee can play an important role in associating both sides of industry in the definition of the Community's economic and social aims.

Above all, vigorous and coordinated action must be taken at Community level to deal with the problem of employment. This will require the Member States, in conjunction with the organizations concerned, to coordinate their employment policies in an appropriate manner and to set priority targets.

26. When the time is ripe, the Council of the Community will consider, in the light of experience and with due regard to the problem of the regions and categories of workers most affected by employment difficulties, whether and to what extent it will be necessary to increase the resources of the Social Fund.

27. Being convinced that in this period of economic difficulty special emphasis should be placed on social measures, the Heads of Government reaffirm the importance which they attach to implementation of the measures listed in the Social Action Programme approved by the Council in its Resolution of 21 January 1974.

28. The Heads of Government make it their objective to harmonize the degree of social security afforded by the various Member States while maintaining progress but without requiring that the social systems obtaining in all Member States should be identical.

Energy

29. The Heads of Government discussed the energy problem and in this connection the related major financial problems created for the Community and for the wider world.

30. They further noted that the Ministers of Energy of the Community countries are due to meet on 17 December.

31. The Heads of Government, aware of the paramount importance which the energy problem has in world economy, have discussed the possibilities for cooperation between oil exporting and oil importing countries, on which subject they heard a report from the Federal Chancellor.

32. The Heads of Government attach very great importance to the forthcoming meeting between the President of the United States and the President of the French Republic.

33. The Heads of Government, referring to the Council Resolution of 17 September 1974, have invited the Community institutions to work out and to implement a common energy policy in the shortest possible time.

Britain's membership of the Community

34. The Prime Minister of the United Kingdom indicated the basis on which Her Majesty's Government approached the negotiations regarding Britain's continued membership of the Community, and set out the particular issues to which the Government attached the highest importance.

35. The Heads of Government recall the statement made during the accession negotiations by the Community to the effect that 'if unacceptable situations were to arise, the very life of the Community would make it imperative for the institutions to find equitable solutions'.

36. They confirm that the system of 'own resources' represents one of the fundamental elements of the economic integration of the Community.

37. They invite the institutions of the Community (the Council and the Commission) to set up as soon as possible a correcting mechanism of a general application which, in the framework of the system of 'own resources' and in harmony with its normal functioning, based on objective criteria and taking into consideration in particular the suggestions made to this effect by the British Government, could

prevent during the period of convergence of the economies of the Member States, the possible development of situations unacceptable for a Member State and incompatible with the smooth working of the Community.

Bulletin of the European Communities, 12. 1974, 7–12

45 Pamphlet opposing continued EEC Membership, issued by the Trades Union Congress of the United Kingdom, May 1975

The trade union movement is against Britain staying in the Common Market. The terms of continuing our membership are damaging to the economy, damaging to industry, and damaging to our democratic freedoms. The Trades Union Congress has spoken out against the terms time after time—when they were first announced by the Conservative Government in 1971, when we were taken into the Market without consultation in 1973, and every year since then. In this year's renegotiations, not enough has been done, not enough has been achieved. As working people prepare to vote in the referendum, the TUC's advice is to vote 'No'. For four good reasons.

Being in the Market means that Britain has to pay more—much more—than its fair share of the Common Market budget. As things stood under the terms Britain went in with, we were to pay 24 per cent of the Common Market's entire budget by 1980—and get back only 14 per cent of the total Common Market income. We were made to buy membership at a high price, and we are being sold short on the benefits. In the renegotiations on our share of the budget, Britain has managed to win agreement from other countries for the Common Market to pay us back up to £125 million a year. But this will still leave us heavily out of pocket—by anything from £175 million to £275 million each year.

The facts are plain: as things stand Britain is going to carry on losing money in the Market. It will be paying out huge sums to other Common Market countries so they can solve their problems of agricultural inefficiency, and it will have too little left to spend on the urgent programme of modernizing our industry, creating more jobs and giving a decent living to pensioners, to the handicapped and the low paid. Just to make matters worse, the system of 'own resources' means that we lose out twice over on food—paying out high taxes for the food we import, and never seeing the money again because it is paying for other countries to improve their agriculture. Tied in with this is the backward, damaging tax system of VAT. It is bad enough as it is, but in future it could get worse, if we are forced to 'harmonize' with other countries, and adopt the same rates as them—perhaps even on necessities.

There is little justice in any of this, you may say. In renegotiation Britain tried to put right the bad terms we went in with—but not enough has been done. The best we can hope for is that from time to time we can persuade the other countries in the Market to treat us as a special case. But it can only be a hope. Not a promise. Certainly not a guarantee. If Britain as a whole is unfairly treated, then working people are doubly mistreated. The guiding principle of the Common Market has been to clear away all obstacles to free competition, and let that rule as a guiding principle in the economy. The twin advances of planning the economy and creating a fairer society—they both go to the wall. Freer movement of capital in Britain has meant freer movement out of Britain—with business finding it easier to dodge its responsibilities to working people, and unions finding it harder to win their programme of social reform.

Being in the Common Market means throwing away a fair and healthy agricultural system—of low food prices and subsidies to farmers—for one based on high prices and free competition. That's the Common Agricultural Policy, which may suit other countries, but it doesn't suit us. Britain—unlike many other European countries—has got a small but efficient farming system, and the food we don't produce for ourselves we have bought from the Commonwealth, and in the world market. It has been a good system. But joining the Common Market has meant fitting in with a policy geared to help other countries by using methods which make us worse off. We have to pay heavily for a system we do not need. The Common Agricultural Policy is aimed at helping farmers by fixing food prices higher than they need to be—often higher than they are in Britain. This encourages surpluses—such as the notorious mountains of butter and beef stockpiled by the Common Market authorities. And it's done by artificially keeping up the cost of imported food with special levies. Maybe it helps other Common Market countries, but it doesn't help us.

It's been said that the basic principles of the Common Agricultural Policy have become more flexible. But that flexibility has been allowed only because of the pressing needs of a particular country—and only as an exception. There is no guarantee that the basic policy will ever be changed permanently, so that a country like Britain can have a policy of its own, suited to its own special needs. It's been said, too, that some world prices are now higher than in the Common Market. That's true, but they're already on the way down now. Yet we still have to buy at Common Market prices. The trade union movement has called for a return to an agricultural policy of our own. After all the renegotiations, it still calls for an agricultural policy of our own.

Being in the Common Market means that the British people no longer have the final say in the way their country is run. Democracy in Britain has been based for centuries on the supreme power of an elected Parliament to pass laws and levy taxes. But this has all been brought into question in the Common Market. Regulations made in Brussels are law in Britain, and they have to be enforced by our courts and put into effect by our administration. But they are not made by the British people, and they are not made by the British Parliament. The trade union movement is deeply concerned that there is no effective democratic check—no arrangement for the will of Parliament to prevail, even in Britain, on the matters covered by laws made under the Treaty of Rome. And it's not just an academic question, either. The laws coming from Brussels can be very detailed, and they can be about bread-and-butter issues affecting everyone. . . .

The Trades Union Congress has called on the Government to give back to Parliament the sole power to pass laws and levy taxes—and this means getting out of the Market, or revising the Treaties wholesale. . . . The Trades Union Congress has rejected union with the Common Market on the present terms, but it has not rejected cooperation between all the countries of Europe on the right basis.

It wants as much as anyone to see political and economic cooperation to achieve goals that can be shared by most countries in Europe, and to go about it in ways they would also agree. The TUC recognizes that today more than ever we need to cooperate in order to raise employment and boost the economy, to curb the rise in prices, to promote social reform, to help developing countries and to meet our common world responsibilities.

And there are actions to back up our words. The TUC is prominent among the trade union movements of the world. It is keeping in close touch with the trade unions of the Commonwealth countries, and it has played a vital role in bringing the trade unions of Europe together by helping to set up the European Trade Union Confedera- tion—which from the very start had more countries in it than the

Common Market, and can speak for nearly all the trade unionists of Western Europe.

The TUC is not turning its back on Europe. It is not isolationist. It is saying that there are things wrong with the Common Market and with the terms as they stand.

Information broadsheet issued by the Trades
Union Congress, May 1975

Reading list

For reference

The Bartholomew/Warne Atlas of Europe. *A profile of Western Europe*, London, 1974.

A. H. Robertson, *European Institutions. Cooperation, Integration, Unification*, London, 1973.

The contemporary world and Europe in general

G. Barraclough, *An Introduction to Contemporary History*, Pelican, 1967.

M. Crouzet, *The European Renaissance since 1945*, London, 1970.

W. Laqueur, *Europe since Hitler*, Pelican, 1970.

J. Major, *The Contemporary World*, London, 1970.

R. Mayne, *The Recovery of Europe*, London, 1970.

M. Pacaut and others, *Le monde contemporain, 1945–1973*, Paris, 1974.

Aspects of European history

P. Ferris, *Men and Money*, Pelican, 1970.

W. Knapp, *Unity and Nationalism in Europe since 1945*, London, 1969.

W. La Feber, *America, Rusia and the Cold War, 1945–1971*, New York, 1971.

R. Morgan, *West European Politics since 1945*, London, 1972.

A. Sampson, *The New Europeans*, Panther, 1971.

The Common Market

Basic Statistics of the Community, Statistical Office of the European Communities.

J. Barber and B. Reed (eds.), *European Community: vision and reality*, London, 1973.

R. C. Mowat, *Creating the European Community*, London, 1973.

W. Hallstein, *Europe in the Making*, London, 1972.

Integration outside the Common Market

J. E. Meade, *Negotiations for Benelux: an annotated chronicle, 1943–56*, Princeton, 1957.

H. Corbet and D. Robertson (ed.), *Europe's Free Trade Area Experiment. EFTA and economic integration*, Oxford, 1970.

A. H. Robertson, *The Council of Europe*, London, 1961.

F. A. Beer, *Integration and Disintegration in NATO*, Ohio, 1969.

M. Kaser, *Comecon. Integration Problems of the Planned Economies*, Oxford, 1967.

S. V. Anderson, *The Nordic Council. A study of Scandinavian regionalism*, Washington, 1967.

Index

208 POST-WAR INTEGRATION IN EUROPE

ECSC—cont.
155; High Authority, 50, 64–7, 151;
Treaty, 50, 60–73, 163
EDC, 4, 50, 51, 56–8, 157
EEC (Common Market), 4, 5, 6, 7, 21, 51,
94, 95, 107, 132, 151, 156–8, 159,
161–2, 163–4, 165–6; Accession Treaty
(1972), 183–5; Associated countries,
87; Commission, 8, 10, 90–91, 170,
178–80, 184; Common Agricultural
Policy, 6, 7, 82–4, 159, 181; Council, 8,
168, 178–80, 184, 199, 200; Court of
Justice, 91, 193; direct elections, 163,
169, 171–3, 182, 196; Economic and
Social Committee, 76, 86, 92, 199;
enlargement, 170, 182–3, 183–5;
European Investment Bank, 75–6, 86;
European Parliament, 6, 7, 8, 87–8,
158, 160, 171–3, 182, 196; European
Social Fund, 75, 182; Luxembourg
agreements, 170, 178–80; merging of
executives, 6, 163; own resources, 163,
181–2, 200; Permanent Representa-
tives, 195; political union, 169, 170,
173–8, 196–7 and see EPC; Summit
Meetings, 169, 170, 174, 180–83,
194–201; Treaty of Rome, 7, 51, 73–93,
101–2, 157, 158, 163, 169, 171, 172,
181, 182, 183, 189–94. See too EDC,
EMU
EFTA, 6, 183; Treaty (of Stockholm), 95,
106–11
Einaudi, Luigi, 11
EMU, 7, 182, 197
EPC, 4, 6, 51
Esperanto, 159
Eurafrica, 156–7
Euratom, 6, 51, 101–2, 156–8, 168, 173,
182, 183–4
European Centre for Nuclear Research
(CERN), 9
European Charter of Education, 9
European Commission, see EEC
European Conference of Ministers of
Transport, 9
European Congress, see Hague Congress
European Cultural Centre, Geneva, 164
European Cup, 9
European Investment Bank, see EEC

European League for Economic Co-
operation (ELEC), 5
European Movement, 5, 21–2, 37–9;
Memorandum of 1962, 151, 162–4,
169; see too Westminster Economic
Conference
European Parliament, see EEC
European Payments Union, 6, 156
European Political Union (Fouchet Plan),
173–8
European Recovery Programme, 3, 21,
22–4, 34, 46–9
European Social Fund, see EEC
European Transport Authority, 6
European Union of Federalists, 5
European University, 182
Eurospace, 9
Eurovision, 9

Faeroes, 119–20
Faure, Maurice, 74
Federal Union, 5
federalism, 1, 5, 10–11, 13–20, 21–2, 35–7
Finland, 5, 94–5, 99, 114–24, 124–30
Ford, Gerald, 198, 200
Fouchet, Christian and the Fouchet Plan,
170, 173–8
France, 1, 3, 4, 7, 8, 10, 11–13, 14, 16, 22,
24, 30, 42, 50–51, 53–6, 58, 60–61,
73–4, 87, 89, 152–6, 159, 160, 167–8,
171, 180, 183; Communist Party, 131;
National Assembly, 50, 56
Franco-German Treaty (1963), 152, 167–8
Frankfurt, 165
French Union, 24, 55

Gasperi, Alcide de, 3, 5, 8
GATT, 107, 186, 198
Gaulle, Charles de, 4, 7, 10; Press
conference (1962), 151, 158–6:
Gaullists, 151, 170
General Motors, 9
Geneva, 10, 11, 12; Peace Congress, 2
German Democratic Republic (East
Germany), 131–44
German Federal Republic (West
Germany), 3, 4, 8, 22, 28, 38, 46, 50–51,
52–5, 56, 58–9, 60–61, 73–4, 131,